LAND YOU CAN HUNT

Other books by BOB GOOCH

Weedy World of the Pickerels
Squirrels and Squirrel Hunting
Bass Fishing
In Search of the Wild Turkey

LAND
YOU CAN HUNT

Bob Gooch

SAN DIEGO • NEW YORK
A. S. BARNES & COMPANY, INC.
IN LONDON:
THE TANTIVY PRESS

The Tantivy Press
Magdalen House
136-148 Tooley Street
London, SE1 2TT, England

For information write to A. S. Barnes and Company, Inc.,
P.O. Box 3051, San Diego, CA 92038

1 2 3 4 5 6 7 8 9   84 83 82 81 80

Library of Congress Cataloging in Publication Data

Gooch, Bob, 1919-
    Land you can hunt.

    Includes index.
    1.   Hunting — United States. I. Title.
SK41.G66   799.2'973   78-75307
ISBN   0-498-02390-7

PRINTED IN THE UNITED STATES OF AMERICA

to Ginny

CONTENTS

Acknowledgments

I am deeply grateful to the information officers of the game agencies in a number of states for their help in the material on their particular states. In most instances, they read the rough draft on their states.

In alphabetical order, they are: Frank P. Hanley of Alabama, Wes Keyes of Arizona, George M. Purvis of Arkansas, George Seymour of California, Richard Hess of Colorado, Greg Sharp of Connecticut, Jim Floyd of Florida, Aaron F. Pass of Georgia, Ronald L. Walker of Hawaii, Jack McNeel of Idaho, James C. Helfrich of Illinois, Wayne Machan of Indiana, Kenneth Formanek of Iowa, George Valyer of Kansas, Bob Dennie of Louisiana, William Jabine of Maryland, Roger Holmes of Minnesota, Joel M. Vance of Missouri, Steve R. Bayless of Montana, Elizabeth V. Huff of Nebraska, William A. Rollins of Nevada, William E. Peterman of New Jersey, Jesse E. Williams of New Mexico, Edward S. Feldman of New York, Duane F. Raver, Jr. of North Carolina, Robert H. Eversole of Ohio, Jim Becker of Oklahoma, Ken Durbin of Oregon, Bob Bell of Pennsylvania, John M. Cronan of Rhode Island, Bob Campbell of South Carolina, Ken Moum of South Dakota, Rich Gilchrist of Tennessee, John Jefferson of Texas, C. Quin Hardin of Utah, Harry L. Gillam of Virginia, Ed Johnson of West Virginia, and Bill Brown of Wyoming.

I would also like to thank the Alaska Department of Fish and Game, the Delaware Division of Fish and Game, the Kentucky Department of Fish and Wildlife Resources, the Maine Department of Inland Fisheries and Wildlife, the Massachusetts Division of Fisheries and Wildlife, the Michigan Department of Natural Resources, the Mississippi Game and Fish Commission, the New Hampshire Fish and Game Department, the North Dakota Game and Fish Department, the Vermont Fish and

Game Department, the Washington Department of Game, and the Wisconsin Department of Natural Resources. Various members of these agencies answered questions and, in most instances, read the rough draft of my manuscript.

Introduction

Over the past twenty years I have hunted dozens of our fifty states.

Each year I go through the same routine, writing first to the appropriate state game agency and following with letters to National Forest supervisors, Bureau of Land Management Offices, and others who administer our vast public lands. Frequently, I go back to the state agency for maps, guides, and other information on specific public hunting areas.

In planning this book, I more or less repeated the process for each of the fifty states. Hopefully, it will save other hunters much of the research, letter writing, delays, and telephone calls I have encountered over the years.

With the wealth of information available today, the hunter can complete much of the planning for a hunt in the comfort of his living room. If he does his homework well, he should arrive in a given state properly licensed, fully advised as to what game is available and what public lands are most promising, up to date on regulations, and headquartered in a convenient campground, hunting lodge, motel, or private home.

Basically, I have described the game species available in each state, with the emphasis on that which is most abundant, and then described the public hunting lands available. Finally, I have attempted to match the game with the best public hunting area.

Admittedly, the value of such a book decreases with the years. Conditions do change, but it has been gratifying to find hunting in many states much as it was as I knew it a decade or more ago. Much of the information is almost ageless.

The hunter desirous of bagging a specific kind of game begins generally with a wide range of possibilities. But the process becomes increasingly difficult right down to the long-awaited shot. Field guides will quickly give him the general range of the game, but he is then faced with the selection of a specific state. Often he has several choices, many of which are equally good. Hopefully, the pages that follow will help him make the correct decision.

Following the selection of a particular state, he must locate the most likely region within it. Here again, he will often have a number of choices, though sometimes only one or two. When they are available, the harvest figures from previous seasons are a good guide.

Once the choice has been made, the book work ends and the actual hunting begins. Hopefully, his research has placed the hunter in the territory where his chances of success are the highest. Now his skills as a hunter take over, and the real joy of hunting begins.

In spite of the yearly increase in "No Hunting" signs, spreading urbanization, new highways, and other inroads of civilization, there is still a vast amount of private and public land open to the hunter in America.

Land You Can Hunt will tell you about it.

B.G
Troy, Virginia

LAND YOU CAN HUNT

1 • ALABAMA—Tops for Turkeys

Alabama's fine turkey hunting, possibly the best in the nation, first lured me to the big Gulf-of-Mexico state, but turkey hunting is just one of the excellent kinds of hunting found in Alabama. Bird hunters take an estimated two million bobwhite quail, and the dove kill is even higher. Small-game hunters will find excellent rabbit and squirrel hunting, and for the big-game hunter, there are good deer herds in addition to turkeys.

Well over three million people live in the state's 51,609 square miles, but there is hunting room for all—and hunting is popular in this big southern state.

In addition to the deer and turkeys, the dove and quail, and the rabbits and squirrels, Alabama offers waterfowl, good populations of woodcocks, snipes, and rails, and raccoons and opossums for the night hunters, and bobcats, foxes, and woodchucks for the varmint man. A good mixture of fox and gray squirrels compose the bushy-tailed populations, though the gray is the most abundant.

The national forests, military lands, and lands of the U. S. Army Corps of Engineers are the Federal contribution to public hunting in Alabama.

The national forests are well distributed throughout Alabama, and provide for hunting just about all of the major game species. Maps can be obtained by writing the U. S. Forest Service Supervisor's Office, 1765 Highland Avenue, Montgomery, AL 36101.

The William B. Bankhead National Forest provides 170,000 acres of public hunting land in the north, and the Talladega National Forest offers another 357,000 acres of fine hunting in the central part of the state. Tuskegee National Forest offers 10,777 acres near Montgomery and 83,770-acre Conecuh National Forest provides public hunting near the Florida border.

Numerous Game and Fish Division wildlife-management areas are located on national forest lands.

Most of the land of the Corps of Engineers is located adjacent to the Corps reservoirs, and information on hunting these areas can be obtained by writing to U.S. Army Corps of Engineers, P.O. Box 2288, Mobile, AL 36601.

Hunting on the various military reservations—Fort Rucker, Fort McClellan, Redstone Arsenal, Fort Benning, and Childersburg Ordinance—is generally limited to military personnel and their guests, but the public is permitted by application on certain hunts.

A fourth Federal agency, the Tennessee Valley Authority, Norris, Tennessee 37828, also has land available for public hunting in Alabama. Write to that address for details.

The very heart of public hunting in the state, however, is a fine system of wildlife-management areas under the supervision of the Game and Fish Division of the Alabama Department of Conservation and Natural Resources. There are now twenty-nine of these well-managed hunting units scattered all over the state. Many are on federal lands, and some are on timber company lands under cooperative agreements with the owners for the management of the game resources. A schedule of these areas, including valuable hunting information, can be obtained by writing to the Department of Conservation and Natural Resources, 64 North Union Street, Montgomery, AL 36130.

The management areas range in size from 216-acre Crow Creek, a waterfowl refuge on the Tennessee River east of Huntsville, to 96,580-acre Black Warrior, a fine deer, turkey, and upland-game area in the William B. Bankhead National Forest. Collectively, they offer over 600,000 acres of good, well-managed, public hunting land. Most are primarily big-game and upland-game lands, but a half dozen offer waterfowl hunting for ducks and geese.

In addition to specific information on individual management areas, the Department of Conservation and Natural Resources can furnish maps of the areas, invaluable tools in planning a hunt. Also available from the same office is an excellent map, State of Alabama Public Hunting Areas, showing the locations of most public hunting lands in the state.

Big timber corporations hold vast tracts of land throughout the state, and much of this land is open to public hunting, though some companies lease the hunting rights to private hunting clubs. Among the major corporations are International Paper Company, Mobile, AL 36601; Gulf States Paper Company, Tuscaloosa, AL 35401; Union Camp Corporation, Chapman, AL 36015; Container Corporation, Brewton, AL 36426; and Great Southern Corporation, Troy, AL 36081. The availability of the lands of these companies for hunting can be determined by writing them at the addresses given.

S. Brooks Holleman and hunting companion Wyatt W. Dawson admire Alabama turkey bagged by Dawson. *Bob Gooch Photo.*

Like the timber company lands, much of the private land in Alabama is tied up in private leases, but the hunter who works at it should be able to gain hunting access to much of it. As in most states, private lands often offer the best hunting, particularly for small game such as rabbits and squirrels, and for birds.

The Alabama posting law is clear, though it treats night hunters a bit differently. Hunting the lands of another without written permission is a misdemeanor. This does not apply to family members, guests, servants, or agents of the landowner, however. A hunter accompanied by the landowner does not need written permission.

The best turkey hunting is found in central and southern Alabama, and on my own hunts in Alabama, I have found the Scotch Wildlife Management Area near the Mississippi border good. This is a big area—20,480 acres. The Conecuh and Talladega National Forests are also good, and many turkeys hunters like the William B. Bankhead National Forest in the northwestern part of the state. Good Wildlife Management Areas, in addition to Scotch, include Barbour, Blue Spring, Butler, Coosa, and Rob Boykin.

All of the national forests are good for deer hunting, though the bulk of the whitetails taken in Alabama come from private lands.

Good quail hunting occurs throughout the state, with the best on private lands, but the edge areas of the national forests and the wildlife-management areas are also fair.

While other forms of hunting are good in Alabama, it is the regal wild turkey that draws most hunters to the big southern state on the Gulf of Mexico.

2 • ALASKA—Every Hunter's Dream

With a population of only 400,000 people and an area of 586,400 square miles—twice the size of Texas—where most of the land is publicly owned, Alaska is truly a hunter's paradise. An Alaskan trip is the dream of most American hunters.

The list of big-game animals is long and impressive. Black bears are abundant, and hunters also take both browns and grizzlies. There are black-tailed sitka deer, a relative of the mule deer, for the deer hunter, and big herds of Barren Ground caribou, the most abundant big-game animal in Alaska. The Alaska moose is the largest found in America, and it ranges over most of the state. Huntable populations of elk live on Afognak and other nearby islands. There is limited hunting for musk ox and a few bison. The mountain-goat hunting is consistently good, and the handsome Dall sheep is the most sought after trophy animal in the state. Wolves and wolverines are classed as big-game animals, and both are abundant. There are a fair number of coyotes, and the lynx populations bounce up and down according to the relative abundance of hares. Both coyotes and lynx are on the game list.

The small-game list is limited to Arctic and snowshoe hares, the red fox, and the red squirrel. Red squirrels are unprotected and rarely hunted.

Various members of the grouse family make up the Alaskan game-bird offering. Present are blue, ruffed, sharp-tailed, spruce, and three ptarmigan—the willow, the rock, and the white-tailed. Ptarmigan are the most abundant of the grouse, but spruce grouse are also plentiful.

While Alaska is a major waterfowl breeding ground, early migrations to the south limit the hunting during much of the long season that opens in September and runs through January. A wide variety of ducks, geese, brant, merganser, sea ducks, snipes, and cranes offer good waterfowl hunting.

Because most land in Alaska is publicly owned, finding a place to hunt is rarely a problem. Hunting on private lands is generally limited to waterfowl, birds, and small game. Few nonresident hunters bother to hunt private lands, but residents encounter little difficulty getting permission to hunt that which is accessible.

Access to the prime game country is more of a problem than locating suitable hunting land. The inexperienced, or hunters new to Alaska, should by all means engage the services of a competent guide or outfitter. A good place to start is the Alaska Professional Hunter's Association, Box 4-1932, Anchorage, Alaska 99509. The membership includes professional guides whose record of ethical conduct is beyond question. Sustaining membership is available to all persons supporting the sport of hunting.

General information on hunting in Alaska can be obtained from the Alaska Department of Fish and Game, Subport Building, Juneau, Alaska 99801. Ask specifically for a copy of the Alaska Game Management Unit Map and Regulations.

While the black bear is abundant in the timbered regions of the southeast, most hunters go to Alaska for browns or grizzlies. Admiralty Island, Kodiak Island, and the Alaska Peninsula are the primary areas for browns, and the Alaska Range, Talkeetna Mountains, and the southern slopes of the Brooks Range are prime grizzly country. By Alaskan law the nonresident hunter must be accompanied by a guide when hunting browns or grizzlies.

One easily accessible caribou herd is that living in the area bounded by the Alaska Range, the Talkeetna Mountains, the Glenn Highway and the Richardson Highway. The caribou in this region are known as the Nelchina herd. This herd and animals from the Alaska Peninsula normally produce the best trophies. Adak Island in the Aleutians also yields some trophy racks.

Moose range almost statewide, but the best trophies come from the Kenai and Alaska Peninsulas. Good trophies may be taken just about anywhere in south central or interior Alaska, however.

The Dall sheep, the white king of the Alaskan mountains, is found in the Wrangell, Chugach and Talkeetna Mountains, the Alaska Range, the Tanana Hills, the Brooks Range, and on the Kenai Peninsula. The best trophies come from the Chugach and Wrangell Mountains and the Alaska Range.

Mountain goats range widely, but live primarily along the coastal

The moose is one of the most popular big-game animals in Alaska. *Alaska Department of Fish and Game photo.*

mountains from Ketchikan to the Kenai Peninsula.

Elk hunting is limited to Afognak Island and nearby Raspberry Island.

The small, black-tailed sitka deer, hunted lightly in Alaska, is primarily an inhabitant of the rain forests of southeastern Alaska, Kodiak Island, and a few islands in Prince William Sound.

Blue grouse inhabit the spruce and hemlock forests of the southeastern part of the state, while spruce grouse are found farther north wherever spruce-birch forests prevail. Ruffed grouse are found in woodlands along the Yukon, Tanana, Kuskokwim and upper Copper Rivers of the interior, and along the Taku and Stikine River drainages. Sharp-tailed grouse live in the Yukon River Valley from Canada to Holy Cross, the Tanana Valley, and in the upper portions of the Koyukuk, Kuskokwim, and Copper River drainages.

Willow ptarmigan occur throughout the state near the timberline where tall spruces give way to alder, willow, and dwarf birch. Rock ptarmigan also live throughout the state, generally in open areas above timberline near dwarf birch, alders, and willows. The white-tailed ptarmigan is restricted to high elevations well above timberline from the Alaska Range south.

Blessed with an abundance of waterfowl, Alaska hunters concentrate on Canada geese, mallards, pintails, and widgeon. There is good waterfowl hunting throughout the state, from Ketchikan to as far north as Barrow.

Arctic hares weighing up to 18 pounds live along the north slope of the Brooks Range and along the entire western margin of the state. Mixed forests, wooded swamps, and brushy areas from sea level to timberline support snowshoe rabbits—just about statewide.

Alaska boasts an abundance of game and almost unlimited public hunting land. Hunting opportunities are boundless, but reaching this rich hunting country is costly, an obstacle many hunters never overcome.

3 • ARIZONA—For Western Quail

Deserts and arid foothills, grassy plateaus, and lofty mountains clothed fascinating squirrel populations characterize Arizona in the colorful Southwest. Big, at 113,000 square miles, it is home to slightly under two million Americans, many of whom hunt and, in general, enjoy their rich outdoor heritage.

Deer abound in Arizona. There are Rocky Mountain mule deer in the mountains, desert muleys in the south, and Coues whitetails in the southeast. The rich western quail family includes the scaled, valley, Mearn's, and Gambel's quails. Efforts are being made to reestablish the masked bobwhite, missing since before the turn of the century because of overgrazing. While the little Abert is the star of the squirrel family, there are also Arizona grays, Kaibab squirrels, Hucahua grays, Apache squirrels, red squirrels, and chickarees. All are not hunted, however.

While deer lead the parade of big-game animals, there are also thriving elk herds, black bears, antelope, bison, javelinas, mountain lions, and wild turkeys. Arizona is one of the few states offering hunting for desert bighorn sheep.

Arizona's excellent quail hunting attracts national attention, but the dove shooting can also be good. Both mourning and white-winged doves are present. Other game birds include chukar partridge, blue grouse, and snipes.

In addition to the excellent squirrel hunting, there are both cottontail and jackrabbits for the small-game hunter, plus fox, coyotes, bobcats, ringtails, raccoons, and a few badgers.

The waterfowl hunting in Arizona is far from spectacular, but there are both ducks and geese, and a handful of waterfowlers enjoy good shooting.

23

Wes Keyes, information officer for the Arizona Game and Fish Department, breaks his state's hunting lands down as follows: Federal ownership—32,255,000 acres, Indian Reservations—19,644,000 acres, state ownership—9,900,000 acres, and private ownership—10,777,000 acres. There are also 314,000 acres of inland waters. Complete hunting information can be obtained from the Arizona Game and Fish Department, 2222 West Greenway Road, Phoenix, Arizona 85023.

Obviously, the federal lands support the bulk of the hunting. Seven national forests blanket 12 million acres of the big southwestern state. They are the Apache and Sitgreaves National Forests, P.O. Box 640, Springerville, AZ 85938; Coconino Forest, P.O. Box 1268, Flagstaff, AZ 86001; Coronado National Forest, Federal Building, 301 Congress Street, Tucson, AZ 85701; Kaibab National Forest, P.O. Box 817, Williams, AZ 86046; Prescott National Forest, P.O. Box 2459, Prescott, AZ 86301; and Tonto National Forest, 102 South 28th Street, Phoenix, AZ 85034. Complete hunting information and excellent maps of these vast areas can be obtained by writing the forest supervisor at the addresses given.

The Bureau of Land Management lands are also vast, and information on them can be obtained from the Bureau of Land Management, 2400 Valley Bank Central, Phoenix, Arizona 85073. The Bureau of Land Management also has excellent maps showing in color code the status of all land in the state. They also include a good deal of general hunting information and pinpoint likely areas for the major game species.

Hunting on the Indian Reservations is subject to the supervision of the tribes. Information is available from the Bureau of Indian Affairs, 124 West Thomas Street, Phoenix, AZ 85013; from the tribes—White Mountain Apache Tribe, P.O. Box 708, Whiteriver, AZ 85941, or San Carlos Tribal Council, P.O. Box "O," San Carlos, AZ 85550; and from the Hualapai Wildlife and Recreation Department, Box 216, Peach Springs, AZ 86434.

While the Arizona Game and Fish Department owns a mere 23,000 acres of land, it is the supervising agency of all wildlife in Arizona according to state law. It is the one to turn to for information on Arizona hunting. The Department can supply information on its own game lands, the huge Kofa and Cabeza Prieta Game Range Refuges, and various waterfowl refuges. The two Game Range Refuges were set aside many years ago to provide protection for the bighorn sheep, hunted today on a limited basis. The Cibola, Havasu, and Imperial Refuges are the major waterfowl refuges. Cibola is managed by the Department, but the other two by the U.S. Fish and Wildlife Service.

The Gambel's quail is a top game-bird in Arizona. *Courtesy of Arizona Game and Fish Department.*

Public land is so abundant in Arizona that there is little reason to hunt on private lands. Still, access to private lands is not often difficult, with the possible exception of those nearest the large cities. The posting law requires the landowner wishing to prohibit hunting to post his land conspicuously at intervals of not more than a quarter of a mile.

Deer hunting is extremely popular in Arizona. The best hunting for the Rocky Mountain mule deer is found in the forested regions. There is good hunting in the vicinity of Flagstaff, Williams, Kingman, and Seligman in the north. The desert mule deer is found primarily in the south, with the best hunting in the vicinity of Tucson and Florence. The whitetail hunting is best in the southeast near the New Mexico border. The Santa Rita Mountains are prime country.

Also popular among big-game hunters is the little javelina. Many nonresident hunters visit Arizona for the specific purpose of hunting the little pig. Possibly the best javelina territory in the state is the region southeast of Tucson. Other good areas include the San Carlos Indian Reservation, the country surrounding Florence, and the foothills east of Phoenix.

Quail hunting is generally best in the southern half of the state. Gambel's quail are abundant in the area between Oracle, Winkelman, and Florence, and in the Tonto Basin. Scaled quail are most abundant in Cochise County, and Mearn's quail hunters will find the oak grasslands of the southeastern mountains good.

Dove hunting is also best in the southern half of the state, much of the very best being close to the Mexican border. Some of the best whitewing shooting in America occurs along the Gila River in the southwestern part of the state. Other good whitewing spots include Arlington, Gila Bend, and Laveen. While mourning doves are more widely distributed, they also concentrate in the grainfields along the Gila River.

A Fish and Game Department survey made several years ago showed the leading squirrel counties were Coconino, Gila, and Yavapai. The very best Abert hunting may be in the Long Valley, Mogollon Rim area of Arizona, however.

Other game species are perhaps less popular generally, but they too have their followers—and are locally popular.

4 • ARKANSAS—For Pin-Oak Mallards

Probably most famous for its waterfowl hunting, Arkansas is also a good deer, quail, and small-game state. An estimated two million people live in its 53,104 square miles.

The whitetail deer is the state's most important big-game animal, yielding an annual harvest of approximately thirty-four thousand animals. The wild turkey is important also, and possibly even more so to the avid turkey man. The estimated turkey population is fifty thousand birds. Wild feral hogs add an interesting bonus for the big-game hunter, but they are not recognized as game animals by the Game and Fish Commission.

The popular bobwhite quail tops the game-bird list, but there is also a rapidly growing interest in the mourning dove, particularly during the migration season. Woodcocks, snipes, and rails round out the game-bird picture.

The squirrel is the top small-game animal in Arkansas, and both the fox and gray squirrels romp in the rich hardwoods of the state. Squirrel habitat is good. Cottontail rabbits are found throughout the state, and the swamp rabbit lives along the streams and bayous. Both gray and red foxes are present and raccoons are abundant, though red foxes are protected. There are also bobcats, woodchucks, and a few coyotes.

The mallard leads the rich parade of waterfowl that use the state, followed by pintails, wood ducks, teal, black ducks, baldpates and gadwalls. Migrating geese include Canadas, blues, snows, and white-fronted geese. The state is famous for its waterfowl hunting.

Cougars, bears, alligators, and red wolves are fully protected.

Much of the hunting in Arkansas is done on private lands, but both federal and state lands offer good public hunting.

Three national forests offer a total of over two and one-half million acres. Included are big Ouachita National Forest, the Ozark National Forest, and small Saint Francis National Forest totaling only 16,000 acres. Write the forest supervisors at Hot Springs, Arkansas 71901, for maps and information on Ouachita, and at Russelville, Arkansas 72801, regarding Ozark and Saint Francis.

Information on various U.S. Army Corps of Engineers lands can be obtained from the Arkansas Game and Fish Commission, Two Capitol Mall, Little Rock, Arkansas 72201. The commission can also furnish information about hunting on the White River National Wildlife Refuge and on other refuges. Regulations vary.

In addition to the federal lands, the commission owns another 300,000 acres of public hunting land. At present, there are thirty such wildlife-management areas ranging in size from 550-acre Seven Devils Swamp to sprawling 34,000-acre Bayou Meto. In comparison to most states, Arkansas's Cooperative Wildlife Management Areas are generally large. Big ones include Sylamore, Piney Creeks, Fort Chaffee, Winona, Muddy Creek, and Caney Creek—all on federal lands.

While deer are found all over the state, the best hunting lies in the south and southeast. Special hunts held on the White River National Wildlife Refuge are usually productive. The three national forests all offer fair to good hunting. Good state-owned, wildlife-management areas include Bayou Meto, Cut-off Creek, Shirey-Rainey, and Bayou De View.

The Winona, Muddy Creek, and Caney Creek Cooperative Wildlife Management Areas, all on national forest lands, provide a high percentage of the total wild turkey harvest. Controlled turkey hunts on the White River National Wildlife Refuge also offer good chances for turkeys.

The state's excellent quail hunting is by far the best on private farmlands, mostly in the southern and eastern regions of the state. However, there is some quail hunting in the national forests, and the Wattensaw, Nimrod, Hope, and Harris Break Wildlife Management Areas are among the best offering fair quail hunting.

There is limited dove hunting on the Hope Wildlife Management Area and a few others, but the best of the dove shooting occurs in the farming areas along the Arkansas and Mississippi Rivers, and in the southern and southwestern regions. Actually, both doves and quail occur in varying degrees of abundance just about all over the state.

Arkansas is famous for its fine waterfowl hunting. *Courtesy of George M. Purvis.*

The cottontail rabbit pretty much roams the state, and the farmlands offer the best hunting, but there is also good cottontail hunting on Petit Jean, Wattensaw, Hope, Cut-off Creek, Francis Sunken Lands, and Seven Devils Swamp Wildlife Management Areas. Sulphur River

Bottoms and Bayou Meto Wildlife Management Areas are good choices for swamp rabbits.

Arkansas is one of the top squirrel-hunting states in America, and the animals are found just about all over the state. All of the well-forested, wildlife-management areas are good, including, among others, Madison County, Big Lake, Hurricane Lake, Black River, and Grassy Lake. The forested river bottoms all over the state are good. The gray squirrel favors the more dense forests, while the bigger fox squirrel shows a decided preference for the edges and wood lots.

Raccoons are plentiful all over Arkansas, preferring much the same kind of timbered bottomlands as the squirrel. Just about all of the public lands, both federal and state, offer good coon hunting.

Foxes, too, occur state-wide, and finding good hunting territory is seldom a problem.

The famed pin-oak flats of the flooded river bottoms are known to avid waterfowlers the world over. Drainage has hurt much of Arkansas's swampy waterfowl country, but duck hunting is still good. Fee hunting is tops in the vicinity of Stuttgart and Dewitt, and much of the hunting is done in this manner, employing top waterfowl guides. The Stuttgart Chamber of Commerce, Stuttgart, Arkansas 72160, can furnish hunting information. Still, there is much excellent public hunting with well over a fourth of the commission's wildlife-management areas flooded each year to attract and hold ducks. There is also a good deal of jump shooting along the state's many fine creeks and rivers.

Listing all of the potential waterfowl hunting areas is impossible here, but good ones includes Big Lake Refuge and Wapanocca, Harris Brake, Nimrod, Petit Jean, Bayou DeView, Shirley Bay-Rainey Brake, Black River, Big Lake, Bayou Meto, Grassy Lake, Sulphur River Bottoms, Seven Devils Swamp, and Saint Francis Sunken Lands Wildlife Management Areas.

There is good public hunting land in Arkansas, but if you decide to hunt the rich private lands, get permission. The Arkansas Game Fish Commission does not enforce the posting law, but the sheriff will!

5 • CALIFORNIA—For Hunting Variety

Both mule- and black-tailed deer, black bears, pheasants, and excellent Pacific Flyway waterfowl hunting make California a top hunting state. The climate runs the gamut from oppressive heat in the canyons to ice and snow in the high country. Big, at 168,693 square miles, California is also populous, with an estimated twenty million people.

The big-game hunter will find mule and black-tailed deer, black bears, wild hogs, and turkeys. Limited hunts for elk and antelope are scheduled as the herds permit. There are also a few mountain sheep, but they are fully protected.

Cottontail rabbits, snowshoe rabbits, jackrabbits, western gray squirrels, a few fox and gray squirrels, bobcats, raccoons, badgers, and gray foxes keep the small-game hunter busy.

The bird hunter is treated to excellent hunting of pheasant, several of the western quail, chukar partridge, sage, blue, and ruffed grouse, band-tailed pigeons, both mourning and white-winged doves, and snipes.

Historically a rich wintering area for ducks and geese, California has possibly the best waterfowl hunting in the Pacific Flyway.

Public hunting land is abundant in California—nineteen national forests, Bureau of Land Management lands, state forests, wildlife refuges, and private lands opened to hunting through cooperative agreements with the California Department of Fish and Game.

National forest lands total over twenty million acres. Maps and information on hunting these lands can be obtained from the forest supervisors. Write Pasadena, CA 91109, for Angeles National Forest; San Diego, CA 92101, for Cleveland National Forest; Placerville, CA 95667, for Eldorado National Forest; Bishop, CA 93514, for Inyo National Forest; Yreka, CA 96097, for Klamath National Forest; Susanville, CA 96130, for Lassen National Forest; Santa Barbara, CA 93102, for Los Padres National Forest; Willows, CA 95988, for Mendocino National Forest; Alturas, CA 96101, for Modoc National Forest; Quincy, CA 95971, for Plumas National Forest; San Bernardino, CA 92403, for San Bernardino National Forest; Porterville, CA 93257, for Sequoia National Forest; Redding, CA 96001, for Shasta National Forest; Fresno, CA 93721, for Sierra National Forest; Eureka, CA 95501, for Six Rivers National Forest; Sonora,CA 95370, for Stanislaus National Forest; Nevada City, CA 95959, for Tahoe National Forest; Redding, CA 96001, and Trinity National Forest; and Reno, NV 89501, for Toiyabe National Forest.

In addition to the national forests, the Bureau of Land Management controls another twelve million acres of land. Much is particularly valuable for bird hunters and small-game hunters. Write the California Department of Fish and Game, 1416 Ninth Street, Sacramento, CA 95814, or the Bureau of Land Management, 650 Capitol Mall, Sacramento, CA 95814, for details.

Military lands on which hunting is permitted include Sierra Ordinance Depot, Herlong, CA 96113; Hunter Liggett Military Reservation, Hunter Liggett, CA 93928; Camp Roberts, Camp Roberts, CA 93446; Fort Ord, Fort Ord, CA 93941; U. S. Naval Ordinance Test Station, China Lake, CA 93557; and U.S. Marine Corps, Camp Pendleton, CA 92055. Write the commanding officer for maps and hunting details.

Hunting is also permitted on many of the national wildlife refuges. Included are Tule Lake, Lower Klamath, Modoc, Clear Lake, Sacramento, Delevan, Colusa, Sutter, Merced, San Luis, Kern-Pixley, and Salton Sea. Write the refuge manager at Route 1, Box 74, Tulelake, CA 96134, for Tule Lake, Lower Klamath and Clear Lake; P.O. Box 1610, Alturas, CA 96101, for Modoc; Route 1, Box 311, Willows, CA 95988, for Sacramento and Delevan; P.O. Box 809, Colusa, CA 95932, for Colusa; P.O. Box 66, Sutter, CA 95932, for Sutter; P.O. Box 854, Merced, CA 95340, for Merced; P.O. Box 2176, Los Banos, CA 93635, for San Luis; P.O. Box 219, Delano, CA 93215, for Kern-Pixley; and P.O. Box 247, Calipatria, CA 92233, for Salton Sea National Wildlife Refuge.

State lands are much more limited and not so necessary with so much federal hunting land. There are four state forests, however—Shasta County, Lake County, Mendocino County, and Tulare County. Write the California Division of Forestry, 1416 Ninth Street, Sacramento, California 95814, for specific information. Additionally, the Department

California hunters enjoy excellent pheasant hunting. *California Department of Fish and Game Photo.*

of Fish and Game owns a number of game-hunting areas that offer everything from waterfowl and small game to birds, turkeys, hogs, antelope, and deer. Among them are Eel River, Biscar, Oroville, Lower Sherman Island, Volta, and Imperial Wildlife Areas. A letter to the department will bring a list of these areas showing their location and the game species present. At present there are sixteen of these well-managed areas.

For information on private lands available under various arrangements, write the Department of Fish and Game. These lands add many additional hunting opportunities. The California trespass law requires the hunter to obtain the permission of the landowner before entering lands under cultivation or fenced, or unenclosed lands where posting signs have been placed at intervals of not less than three to a mile.

Of the various species of mule and black-tailed deer, the blacktail is the most abundant with the best hunting between the Oregon border and Santa Barbara County and along the western slope of the Sierra Cascade Range. Good counties include Humboldt, Mendocino, Shasta, and Trinity. Both the national forests and the Bureau of Land Management lands offer good deer hunting.

Black bears are found mostly in the northwestern quarter of the state and in the interior mountains. Good counties include Humbolt, Shasta, and Siskiyou.

Monterey County is probably the best spot for wild hogs, and San Luis Obispo County is the usual choice of turkey hunters.

The best pheasant hunting is found on private lands, mostly in the Sacramento Valley, the northern regions of the Delta area, and in the San Joaquin Valley.

The California, Gambel's, and mountain quail provide excellent quail hunting, with the California the most abundant. The coastal foothills offer good hunting for California or valley quail, and San Bernardino, Riverside, and Imperial Counties are tops for Gambel's. The western slope of the Sierras is recommended for mountain quail.

Fresno, Kern, and Inyo are good chukar counties.

The large interior valleys in the southern part of the state offer the best dove hunting.

The bulk of the Pacific Flyway waterfowl harvest comes from California, long a top waterfowl state. Both the national wildlife refuges and the state waterfowl-management areas offer duck and goose shooting under a permit system. Applications for permits are available from license agents or from the Department of Fish and Game.

Californians are appreciative of their vast hunting lands—and rightly so.

6 • COLORADO—For Elk and Muleys

Big—104,247 square miles—and high—14,431 feet with 53 mountain peaks in excess of 14,000 feet—Colorado is a top big-game state, one of the few offering ptarmigan hunting, and a rugged state rich in wilderness and wildlife.

Colorado is one of the truly great mule deer states, and its impressive elk herds have drawn hunters to its high country for generations.

Approximately a third of the state's land is in public ownership, and there is very little privately owned land in the high country west of Denver.

Mule deer hunters bag over sixty thousand animals annually, and elk hunters do well with a harvest in the neighborhood of twenty thousand. Antelope are abundant in the big plains country east of Denver, with the success ratio averaging well above seventy percent. The black-bear hunting is reasonably good, but grizzlies are completely protected. Bighorn sheep and mountain goats are limited to resident hunters. A few buffalo and mountain lions round out the big-game species.

Wild turkeys are also hunted.

While it is the state's rich big-game hunting that attracts hunters from distant points, many hunters prefer the varied bird hunting. Pheasants lead the parade with an annual harvest of approximately 125,000 ringnecks. The scaled quail is the most abundant of the three species of quail, followed by the Gambel's and the bobwhite.

Blue grouse are reasonably abundant in the mountain forests, and hunters bag an estimated ten thousand sage grouse annually. There are a few sharp-tailed grouse, and introduced chukars are fairly well established. White-tailed ptarmigan are found mostly above the timberline, and they offer fair sport for experienced hunters. Mourning doves are reasonably abundant.

Small game includes the cottontail rabbit, snowshoe hare, and both white-tailed and black-tailed jackrabbits. There are a few fox squirrels and some Abert squirrels which are protected. Bobcats, coyotes, and foxes add interest to the total hunting picture.

The Continental Divide, which splits the state, also divides it into two flyways, the Central and the Pacific, so the waterfowl regulations vary. The waterfowl hunting is excellent, however, with mallards the major species. The goose hunting is superb, and there is limited hunting for sand-hill cranes.

With more than fourteen million acres of the state in eleven national forests, there is no shortage of public hunting land. The national forests are the backbond of the state's fine big-game hunting.

The White River National Forest, with almost two million acres, is the largest and one of the best for mule deer and elk. Headquarters are at Glenwood Springs, Colorado 81601. Write there for maps and hunting information. Other large National Forests include San Isabel, headquartered at Pueblo, CO 81001; Routt, headquartered at Steamboat Springs, CO 80477; San Juan, headquartered at Durango, CO 81301; Rio Grande, headquartered at Monte Vista, CO 81144; Pike, headquartered at Pueblo, CO 81001; Routt, headquartered at Steamboat Gunnison, CO 81230; and Arapaho, headquartered at Golden, CO 80401. The Grand Mesa and Uncompahgre are headquartered at Delta, CO 81416, and Roosevelt National Forest is headquartered at Fort Collins, CO 80521.

Several of the national forests contain wilderness and primitive areas from which all vehicular traffic is prohibited. These are often game-rich areas worthy of consideration. Maps of the wilderness and primitive areas can be obtained from the Denver Federal Center, Building 85, Denver, Colorado 80225.

Not to be overlooked are over eight million acres of land administered by the Bureau of Land Management. These lands generally lie at lower elevations than the national forests and are scattered throughout the state. Many tracts are located on the broad eastern plains. They offer hunting for mule deer, antelope, game birds, and small game. An excellent map showing the location of the Bureau of Land Management lands can be obtained from the Bureau of Land Management State Office, 16th at Broadway, Denver, Colorado 80202.

In addition to the vast Federal lands, the Colorado Division of Wildlife, 6060 North Broadway, Denver, Colorado 80216, owns or ad-

Colorado is one of the top elk-hunting states. *Courtesy of Don Domenick.*

ministers another 250,000 acres of hunting and fishing areas. Of varying sizes, they offer both large and small game hunting. A complete list of these areas, showing their location and describing the hunting they offer, can be obtained from the above address.

While there is a fair amount of private land open to public hunting, it has decreased drastically in recent years because of the tremendous hunting pressure that state's game has been subjected to. Still, access to much of it is there for the asking.

Colorado's posting law is a tough one. While "No Hunting" signs are prevalent, particularly in areas adjacent to the national forests, the landowner is not required to post his land. The hunter who enters it without permission is automatically guilty of trespass. Permission can be verbal, however.

Mule-deer and elk hunters will like Colorado. The herds are large and healthy, and hunting country is spacious. Even so, the hunter will encounter many fellow nimrods unless he packs deep into the back country.

Guides are not a legal requirement, but a good guide's knowledge of the country and game conditions can increase a hunter's chances tremendously. Still, many experienced hunters run their own show and enjoy high success.

Mule deer are found all over the state, but the high country to the west of Denver, the national forests, and Bureau of Land Management lands offer by far the best hunting.

Elk hunters, too, will find their chances of success highest on the vast western slope.

Hunting opportunities for both deer and elk are numerous. From personal experience, I have found the White River National Forest south of Silt good, but this is just one of many prime areas. Game conditions vary from season to season, however.

Antelope are concentrated in the eastern plains regions, and black bears are found just about everywhere in the western forests and mountains.

For the bird hunter, Colorado can provide the unusual in hunting for ptarmigan and blue grouse. Both live at high altitudes—the grouse in the forests and ptarmigan above timberline. The National Forest high country is the place to look for these members of the grouse family.

Colorado's dry sagebrush flats also offer some of the best sage-grouse hunting in America, though it is not really good anywhere today.

An autumn hunt in Colorado's high country when the quaking aspens are trimmed in gold, and the nights are cold but the days brisk can be much more than a highly successful hunt. It can be an outdoor experience you will not soon forget.

7 • CONNECTICUT—For Birds and Small Game

With a population of three million people crowded into 5,009 square miles, Connecticut's game resources probably receive as much hunting pressure as any in the United States. Still, there is reasonably good hunting for those who are willing to work for it. Slightly over 100,000 acres of high land and another 14,000 acres of marshland are open to public hunting.

The white-tailed deer is the only big-game animal in the state, and hunting for it is extremely limited. On the public hunting areas, the deer hunter is restricted to the shotgun, muzzle-loader, or bow and arrow.

Small game includes both cottontail and snowshoe rabbits, gray squirrels, raccoons, foxes, and woodchucks.

The pheasant is the most important game bird, but there are also bobwhite quail, woodcocks, ruffed grouse, chukar partridge, rails, and snipes. Crow hunters enjoy a split season.

The waterfowl hunting is reasonably good and the duck hunters may well enjoy the cream of the hunting in this crowded New England state.

There are no national forests or other federal lands in Connecticut, so the hunter must rely upon state, local government, and private lands for hunting. Those who know the state well enjoy reasonably good hunting on such lands.

State forests provide 122,480 acres of public hunting land. The largest is 22,937-acre Pachaug State Forest, located in eastern Connecticut. Another large one is Cockaponset State Forest, located in the central part of the state. The American Legion State Forest of 782 acres is one of the smallest, but most are in excess of 1,000 acres.

Wildlife-management areas add another forty thousand acres of public hunting land, all of which is managed specifically for game and other forms of wildlife. Finally, there are another fourteen thousand acres of waterfowl marshlands open to public hunting.

Complete information on these areas can be obtained by writing or calling the Connecticut Department of Environmental Protection, State Office Building, 165 Capitol Avenue, Hartford, CT 06115.

Deer hunting is best in the western counties and in the far northeastern corner of the state. With hunters limited to the shotgun, muzzle-loader, or bow and arrow, the hunting is broken down into three categories.

Big Housatonic State Forest is one of the top deer-hunting areas in Connecticut, but there is also deer hunting in Mattatuck, Naugatuck, Wyantenock, Paugusett, Upper Paugussett, Wyantenock, Cockaponset, Nassahegon, Nepaug, Tunxis, Peoples, Nye Holman, Salmon River, Nehantic, Shenipsit, Natchaug, Nipmuck, and Pachaug State Forests. Bartlett Brook and Wopowog Wildlife Management Areas also offer deer hunting.

The ruffed grouse may be the best bet for the serious bird hunter in Connecticut who prefers true wild birds. The hardy birds are found in the Housatonic, Mattatuck, Naugatuck, Wyantenock, Paugusett, Cockaponset, Nassahegon, Nepaug, Tunxis, Peoples, Nye Holman, Salmon River, Nehantic, Shenipsit, Nathan Hale, Natchaug, Nipmuck, and Pachaug State Forests; in the Mansfield Hunting Area; and in Wangunk, Wopowog, Pease Brook, Assekonk Swamp, Barn Island, Bartlett Brook, and Rose Hill Wildlife Management Areas.

Probably second in importance to the birdhunter is the woodcock. Good state forests include Housatonic, Mattatuck, Naugatuck, Wyantenock, Paugussett, Cockaponset, Nye Holman, Salmon River, Nathan Hale, Natchaug, Nipmuck, and Pachaug. Also worth checking out are Cromwell Meadows, Durham Meadows, Dr. John E. Flaherty, Mansfield Hunting Area, Wangunk Meadows, Pease Brook, Assekonk Swamp, Barn Island, Franklin Swamp, Bartlett Brook, and Rose Hill Wildlife Management Areas.

Pheasants are found in the Housatonic, Naugatuck, Wyantenock, Paugussett, Nye Holman, Salmon River, Nathan Hale, Natchaug, and **Pachaug State Forests, and on the Simsbury, Cromwell Meadows,** Durham Meadows, Dr. John E. Flaherty, Mansfield Hunting Area, Wangunk Meadows, Wopowog, Pease Brook, Assekonk Swamp, Barn Island, Franklin Swamp, Bartlett Brook, and Rose Hill Wildlife Management Areas.

There is good rail hunting in the Charles E. Wheeler, Cromwell

The author with a Connecticut ruffed grouse. *Photo by Ginny Gooch.*

Meadows, Ragged Rock, Great Island, and Lord's Cove Wildlife Management Areas.

Quail hunting is probably best on private lands, but there is some hunting on the Dr. John E. Flaherty, Barn Island, and Bartlett Brook Wildlife Management Areas.

The Charles E. Wheeler, Cromwell Meadows, Ragged Rock, Great

Island, and Lord's Cove Wildlife Management Areas are good bets for rails and snipes.

Rabbits are the most popular small game in Connecticut, and the cottontail is found just about all over the state where there is suitable habitat. The Housatonic, Mattatuck, Naugatuck, Wyantenock, Paugussett, Nassahegon, Nepaug, Tunxis, Peoples, Cockaponset, Nye Holman, Nehantic, Shenipsit, Nathan Hale, Natchaug, and Pachaug State Forests provide hunting for cottontails. There are also rabbits on Simsbury, Durham Meadows, Dr. John E. Flaherty, Wangunk Meadows, Wopowog, Pease Brook, Assekonk Swamp, Barn Island, Franklin Swamp, Bartlett Brook, and Rose Hill Wildlife Management Areas.

Snowshoe hares, not truly abundant in the state, can be found in Tunxis, Peoples, Nipmuck, and Pachaug State Forests.

The gray squirrel is also popular among small-game hunters, and all of the state forests support good populations of bushy-tails. Good squirrel hunting can also be found on the Cromwell Meadows, Durham Meadows, Mansfield Hunting Area, Wangunk Meadows, Wopowog, Barn Island, and Bartlett Brook Wildlife Managaement Areas.

Raccoons are found in the Housatonic, Mattatuck, Naugatuck, Wyantenock, Paugussett, Cockaponset, Nassahegon, Nepaug, Tunxis, Peoples, Nipmuck, and Pachaug State Forests, and in the Bartlett Brook, Wopowog, and Wangunk Meadows Wildlife Management Areas.

And try the Housatonic, Wyantenock, Cockaponset, Tunxis, Peoples, Natchaug, and Pachaug State Forests for waterfowl. Better still, try Bartlett Brook, Barn Island, Assekonk Swamp, Wangunk Meadows, Lord's Cove, Great Island, Mansfield Hunting Area, Ragged Rock, Great Harbor, Durham Meadows, Cromwell Meadows, Charles E. Wheeler, and Simsbury Wildlife Management Areas. Among them may be the very best hunting in Connecticut.

8 • DELAWARE—For Ducks

With a population of half a million people living in three counties totaling only 2,057 square miles, it could reasonably be assumed that there is no room for the hunter in this small state on the Atlantic Coast. But twelve percent of those 2,057 square miles are marshlands, and the highest elevation is only 450 feet. Waterfowl hunting can be very good, though the state depends upon the migratory birds of the Atlantic Flyway for its ducks and geese.

Both the Division of Fish and Wildlife and private landowners attempt to hold ducks and geese in the state. They succeed to a degree, but must look to the Flyway to sustain the excellent hunting Delaware waterfowlers enjoy.

While the major emphasis is on the fine waterfowl, the state offers a variety of other hunting opportunities.

The quail hunting can be very good, though it is limited and mostly on private lands. There is fair pheasant hunting, but it is mostly a put-and-take affair, with the birds released on suitable public lands. The dove hunting is good, and there is fair woodcock hunting during the fall migration. Snipes, rails, coots and gallinules round out the game-bird offering.

The big-game hunter is limited to deer, but whitetail hunters fare well, bagging 750 to 1,000 animals annually. The shotgun and the bow and arrow are the only legal weapons.

Small-game hunters enjoy good rabbit and squirrel hunting, and foxes, raccoons, and opossums provide sport for the hound man. Woodchucks are fairly abundant in the farming regions. Squirrel and woodchuck hunters may use rifles.

Federal lands in Delaware are limited to those administered by the

The author with a good bag of ducks taken over the Delaware marshes. *Photo by Ginny Gooch.*

U.S. Fish and Wildlife Service as refuges for waterfowl. There are only two refuges, but between them, they provide almost as much public land as does the Delaware Division of Fish and Wildlife. Bombay Hook Refuge in Kent County on the coast contains approximately 15,000 acres of marshlands, and to the south, in Sussex County there is Prime Hook Refuge. Information on hunting these areas can be obtained by writing to the Refuge Manager, Bombay National Wildlife Refuge, R.D.#1, Box 147, Smyrna, DE 19977, and the Refuge Manager, Prime Hook National Wildlife Refuge, R. D. #1, Milton, DE 19968.

Wildlife areas owned by the Delaware Division of Fish and Wildlife contain in excess of 20,000 acres of prime hunting land. There are over a dozen scattered throughout the state, and among them, they provide hunting for every kind of game found in the state. A list of these areas and complete hunting information, including maps, can be obtained by writing the Delaware Department of Natural Resources and Environmental Control, Division of Fish and Wildlife, Dover, DE 19901.

All of the Wildlife Areas except Reedy Island in the Delaware River provide deer and small-game hunting. There are a half-dozen waterfowl wildlife areas, and another nine which are stocked with ring-necked pheasants.

Three state forests, Blackbird, Ellendale, and Redden, provide another 6,000 acres of small-game and deer hunting lands. Information on these can also be obtained from the Division of Fish and Wildlife at the above address.

As is true in many eastern states, the best hunting for many species, particularly deer, doves, quail, and waterfowl, is usually found on private lands. Permission to hunt deer, doves, quail, and small game can be obtained by politely approaching the landowner.

The Delaware posting law is simple and tough. It is unlawful to trespass with gun or dog without the permission of the landowner, and north of the Chesapeake and Delaware Canal, it is unlawful to discharge weapons without the written permission of the landowner.

The best quail hunting in Delaware is probably found on the farm lands of Kent and Sussex Counties near the Maryland line. Both the Petersburg and Milford Neck Wildlife Areas offer fair quail hunting, and there is reasonably good hunting in the Redden State Forest.

The same general area offers the best dove hunting in the state.

Both of the national wildlife refuges offer fair woodcock hunting, as do the Canal, Blackiston, and Petersburg Wildlife Areas, but the migrating birds are likely to be found anywhere there are wet areas in the upland country.

The deer hunting is best in the central portion of Delaware, and the wildlife areas in that section offer the best public hunting.

Rabbits and squirrels are found throughout the state, and the best hunting is often found on private lands. The Canal Wildlife Area offers almost five thousand acres of reasonably good squirrel and other small-game hunting.

The Canal Wildlife Area is probably also the best public pheasant hunting territory in Delaware, though any of those designated for pheasant hunting should be reasonably good as they are stocked with pen-raised birds, the only kind of pheasant hunting generally available in the state.

Delaware game managers do a remarkable job of maintaining good game resources in the face of tremendous pressure.

9 • FLORIDA—Deer and Turkeys and Doves and Quail

Mostly subtropical, with a climate that is seldom harsh, Florida is an interesting and productive hunting state. Over six million people live in its generally flat 58,560 square miles.

The big-game hunter will find good white-tailed deer hunting with the animals very abundant in some regions, some of the best turkey hunting in America, large and ferocious feral hogs, and a few black bears.

Doves and quail are the major game birds, and the annual harvest for each runs into the millions. There are a few woodcocks, snipes are reasonably plentiful, and there is an abundance of rails and gallinules.

Florida has an abundance of gray squirrels, a few fox squirrels, and an abundance of cottontail, marsh, and swamp rabbits. Raccoons are sometimes overly populous. Other animals include both gray and red foxes, opossums, and a few bobcats.

Rich in coastal waters, marshes, rivers, and inland lakes, Florida is a top waterfowl hunting state. A wide variety of ducks make the state attractive to waterfowlers generally.

Three national forests provide the bulk of the federal lands in Florida, but there are also military reservations and other federal lands. Information and maps on the military reservations and the federal lands can be obtained from the Florida Game and Fresh Water Fish Commission, 620 South Meridian, Tallahassee, Florida 32304.

At 556,480 acres, Apalachicola National Forest is the largest of the three. Osceola in the northeast has 361,029 acres, and Ocala National Forest offers 157,233 acres of public hunting lands. Maps and hunting information on the national forests is available from the Forest

Supervisor, Florida National Forests, Tallahassee, Florida 32302. Hunting is generally prohibited in the famous Everglades National Park at the southern tip of Florida; however, there is good waterfowl hunting on the Chassahowitzka, Loxahatchee, St. Marks, and Merritt Island National Wildlife Refuges. Write the commission for details.

Possibly of more importance to the hunter than even the big national forests are the well-managed, wildlife-management areas of the Game and Fresh Water Fish Commission. There are forty-three of them scattered at strategic locations over the state. They vary in size from Apalachee Wildlife Management Area, which will support an estimated two hundred hunters, to big Apalachicola, which can accomodate eight thousand. The Game and Fresh Water Fish Commission has excellent maps of each of the areas. These maps also contain valuable information as to seasons, legal game, and regulations.

The state's Dove Fields Program, which offers over seventy such hunting areas, is particularly popular.

Other state-owned lands include flood-control districts, state forests, and other agency lands, most of which are open as cooperative public hunting areas and run as wildlife-management areas.

Timber companies such as St. Joe Paper Company, Buckeye Cellulose Company, Canal Timber Company, Container Corporation of America, Owens-Illinois, Inc., Miami Corporation, Ocala Lumber Sales Company, Hudson Pulp and Paper Company, Florida Power and Light Company, St. Regis Paper Company, Union Camp, and others provide millions of acres of hunting land, much of it open to the public as wildlife-management areas. The Game and Fresh Water Fish Commission can supply information on these lands.

There is also a good deal of excellent hunting on private farms and ranch lands, but the permission of the owner is required before entering such lands.

All of the national forests and many of the wildlife management areas offer good hunting for white-tailed deer. Fisheating Creek, Aucilla, Everglades, Lake Butler, and Tomoka are good wildlife-management areas.

Bear hunting is currently limited to Baker and Columbia Counties. Special hunts are held in the Apalachicola and Osceola National Forests.

Wild hogs are legal in designated areas each season. Good wildlife-management areas include Aucilla, Apalachicola, Robert Brent, Everglades, and Cecil M. Webb. The three national forests all offer good turkey hunting, but the big Fisheating Creek Wildlife Management Area is one of the best regions in the state.

Spring turkey hunting is popular among Florida hunters. *Courtesy of Lovett Williams, Jr.*

While the best quail hunting is probably found on private lands, there is good bobwhite hunting on the wildlife-management areas. Good ones include St. Regis, Gaskin, Cecil M. Webb, Apalachee, and Avon Park. There is also good quail hunting on the Elgin Air Force Base.

The Dove Fields Program areas are the best bet for dove hunting, and

Florida is one of the top mourning dove states. The Game and Fresh Water Fish Commission can supply information on the location of these fields and the shooting dates. They are not hunted every day. Good wildlife-management areas include Aucilla, Croom, Avon Park, and Apalachee. Apalachee Wildlife Management Area also offers a fair amount of woodcock hunting, and Avon Park, Croom, and the Guano River Wildlife Management Areas offer fair hunting for snipes. Rails are abundant in the salt and fresh water marshes all over the state. The clapper lives in the salt marshes, and the king lives in the fresh water marshes.

The three national forests offer prime squirrel hunting, but there is also some good hunting on the wildlife-management areas. Good ones include Aucilla, Croom, Fisheating Creek, Guano River, Point Washington, and Richloam.

Rabbits are so plentiful throughout Florida that there is no closed season on them. They can be found just about anywhere, though the marsh and swamp rabbits are limited to the low, wet areas. Apalachee, Blackwater, Bull Creek, Fort McCoy, Green Swamp, Ocala, Steinhatchee, and the Tides Swamp are just a few of the Wildlife Management Areas that offer good rabbit hunting. Raccoons and opossums are found all over the state also, and good wildlife-management areas for coons, possums, foxes, and bobcats include Croom, Nassau, Gaskin, Blackwater, Apalachicola, Ocala, Cypress Creek and the Elgin Air Force Base.

The Chassahowitzka, Loxahatchee, and St. Marks Waterfowl Refuges, and Merritt Island National Wildlife Refuge offer public hunting, but the wildlife-management areas are a better choice generally for the waterfowl hunter. Good ones include Apalachee, Corbett, Fisheating Creek, Ft. McCoy, Ocala, Everglades, and Guano River. There is also a good bit of jump shooting along the rivers and streams.

Perhaps better known for its excellent fishing, Florida has much to offer the hunter.

10 • GEORGIA—For Bobwhites

Probably some of the best, or the very best, bobwhite-quail hunting in America can be found in Georgia, though most of it is on private lands. Often called the Quail Capital of the World, Georgia offers top bobwhite hunting, some of it on lands open to the public.

Georgia has an area of 58,876 square miles and a population of four and one-half million people. Finding a place to hunt in Georgia can sometimes be a problem, but a knowledge of the public and private lands on which public hunting is permitted can help alleviate the problem.

The dove is the state's most popular game bird, though Georgia is noted for its quail hunting. The annual harvest far exceeds that of quail. The quail hunting, however, ranks with the best to be found anywhere. There is some fair ruffed-grouse hunting in the mountains of northern Georgia, but typical of southern grouse hunting, it is tough and physically demanding. Woodcocks are scattered generally throughout the state, but the woodcock is not an important game bird. The hunting for both king and clapper rails is good along the coast, and a smattering of snipes rounds out the game-bird picture in Georgia.

The big-game hunter will find excellent deer hunting, wild turkeys on the increase again, and feral hogs. The hogs are domestic animals that have taken up life in the wild. They are not considered game animals, but many hunters find them a tough and challenging quarry.

Both gray and fox squirrels, and cottontail, swamp, and marsh rabbits lead the parade of excellent small game animals in Georgia. All are abundant. There are plenty of raccoons and opossums for the night hunters, and foxes are abundant and unprotected.

While Georgia is not a top waterfowl state, there is reasonably good hunting along the coast and on the inland lakes. Jump shooting along the inland rivers is popular among many local hunters. The three federal wildlife refuges are a boon to waterfowlers.

Federal lands are significant in the state. The Chattahoochee and Oconee National Forests provide a total of 781,700 acres of fine hunting land, much of which is managed by the Georgia Game and Fish Division for wildlife. Maps and hunting on these two National Forests can be obtained from the Forest Supervisor, U.S. Forest Service, Gainesville, Georgia 30501. The military lands in the state make a substantial contribution to the public hunting opportunities. Both Fort Stewart and Fort Benning are open to public hunting, but Dobbins, Glynco and Warner Robbins Air Force Bases are generally limited to base personnel. Hunting information can be obtained by writing the provost marshall of the military reservations, or the Georgia Department of Natural Resources, Trinity-Washington Building, 270 Washington Street, S.W., Atlanta, Georgia 30334. Federal lands also include three wildlife refuges — Blackbeard Island Refuge and Savannah Refuge, with the Refuge Manager at Route 1, Hardeeville, South Carolina 29927, and the Piedmont Refuge, with the Refuge Manager at Round Oak, Georgia 31080.

Georgia's wildlife-management-area system, under the jurisdiction of the Department of Natural Resources, has opened up more than one and one-half million acres of prime hunting land to the public. It is the very heart of public hunting in the state and makes available to the average hunter just about every species of game found in Georgia. There are forty of these fine hunting areas scattered throughout the state. Information on the Wildlife Management Areas can be obtained from the Department of Natural Resources.

An even greater amount of hunting land is owned by private timber companies. Their combined acreage totals three million, and many of these acres are open to public hunting. The major companies are Armstrong Cork, P.O. Box 4288, Macon, GA 31208; Brunswick Pulp and Paper Company, Brunswick, GA 31520; Champion International, P.O. Box 667, Washington, GA 30673; Container Corporation of America, North Eighth Street, Fernandina Beach, FL 32034; Georgia Kraft Company, P.O. Box 1551, Rome, GA 30161; Gilman Paper Company, St. Marys, GA 31558; Great Northern Paper Company, P.O. Box 44, Cedar Springs, GA 31732, International Paper Company, Georgetown, SC 29440; ITT Rayonier, Inc., P.O. Box 528, Jesup, GA 31545, Kimberly-Clark, Washington, GA 30673; and Union Camp Corporation, P.O. Box 570, Savannah, GA 31402. Write these

Georgia is one of our oldest and best bobwhite-quail states. *Courtesy of Aaron F. Pass.*

corporate offices for information on hunting their lands.

The Georgia posting law makes it illegal to hunt on private lands without first obtaining the permission of the landowner.

The white-tailed deer, the major big-game animal in Georgia, is found just about statewide, but the best hunting is in the middle of the state. Cedar Creek, Central Georgia Branch Station, Ocmulgee, West Point, and Whitesburg Wildlife Management Areas are good possibilities. The wild turkey, still in the recovery stage in the state, is found principally in the eastern counties.

The best of the quail hunting is found on private lands, usually the big plantations, but there is some public hunting on the wildlife management areas. Good ones include Alapaha, Bullard Creek, Baldwin State Forest, and, to a lesser degree, Lake Russell and Talkin Rock.

Dove hunting is best on private lands, also, but Albany Nursery, Grand Bay, Ocmulgee, and Allatonna Wildlife Management Areas offer some good dove shooting.

Cohutta, Coleman River, Blue Ridge, and Warwoman Wildlife Management Areas offer good grouse hunting, as does the Chattahoochee National Forest, generally.

There is reasonably good squirrel hunting on just about every wildlife-management area. Both national forests are good and so are the millions of acres of private land on which public hunting is permitted. Fox squirrels are found mostly in central and south Georgia. The more abundant gray occurs statewide. Rabbits are found statewide also, but the best hunting is probably on the farmlands where the permission of the owner is required. The great majority of the wildlife-management areas in middle and south Georgia offer some rabbit hunting.

Raccoons and opossums are found just about all over the state. The Blue Ridge, Chattahoochee, Chestatee, Cohutta, Talking Rock, and Warwoman Wildlife Management Areas are among those open to coon hunting on specified nights. Racoons are more abundant in the southeastern part of the state. Foxes are found all over Georgia, but the best hunting is on private lands.

The best waterfowl hunting in Georgia is along the coast, with good hunting on the Lake Seminole and Altamaha Wildlife Management Areas. There is some hunting on inland beaver ponds, found mostly on private property.

Plains, Georgia, makes the national headlines, but the state's hunting is also worthy of note.

11 • HAWAII—Six Islands of Hunting

Hawaii, our fiftieth state and the only one outside of the continental United States, offers a wide variety of hunting — hunting unlike that found anywhere else in America. Eight major islands comprise this state, and hunting is permitted on six of them.

Current hunting regulations list fifteen species of game birds and seven game animals, a truly rich variety of hunting. Such exotic species as axis deer, mouflon, barred and lace-necked doves, francolins, and Barbary and bamboo partridge suggest hunting in faraway lands, but actually it is reasonably convenient and available to most Americans.

The major islands that make up the State of Hawaii are Hawaii, the "big island," Kahoolawe, Kauai, Lanai, Maui, Molokai, Nihau, and Oahu, the home of Honolulu, the state capital. Kauai and Nihau are located to the northwest of Oahu, and the remainder are to the southeast.

Hunting is permitted on the Islands of Hawaii, Kauai, Lanai, Maui, Molokai, and Oahu.

The famous Hawaiian climate ranges from subtropical to subalpine. The terrain is also widely varied—flat to rocky and steep, with rain forests, open parklands, and open-to-dense dry forests.

The eight major islands total 6,450 square miles and have a population of 788,000 people.

Military lands, the Hawaii National Park, and National Wildlife Refuges make up the bulk of the federal lands in Hawaii. The Hawaiian Islands National Wildlife Refuge and the Haleakala National Park are examples of areas set aside for wildlife, but hunting is limited or totally prohibited.

On the other hand, the Hawaii Division of Fish and Game does

Hawaii, the Island State, offers hunting for exotic game. *Hawaii Division of Fish and Game Photo.*

control vast areas of highly varied land that is available for public hunting, and it is toward this land that the hunter should direct his attention. Many of the public hunting lands are owned by private interests or other public agencies, but hunting is controlled by the Division of Fish and Game.

The Division of Fish and Game has separate regulations applying to each of the six islands on which hunting is permitted. Handy division bulletins include current regulations, descriptions of the individual hunting areas, game species, and sketch maps of the areas. The maps also show the location of the particular island in relation to the other seven in the chain.

The bulletin covering the Island of Molokai, for example, lists hunting units one through seven, describes the individual units, and locates them on the map. The map also shows the location of the island as being between Oahu and Lanai.

Like bulletins are available for the other five islands on which hunting is permitted. Hunting lands are most abundant on the islands of Hawaii, Kauai, and Lanai.

Complete information on hunting these lands can be obtained by writing the Hawaii Division of Fish and Game, 1151 Punchbowl Street, Honolulu, Hawaii 96813.

Game-management areas and forest reserves support the bulk of the public hunting in Hawaii. There are an estimated one million acres of forest reserves, many of which are open to public hunting. The Division of Fish and Game can also supply information on these lands.

The permission of the landowner is required before entering private lands, and while the law does not require it, the Division of Fish and Game recommends playing it safe by obtaining written permission.

Axis deer, wild goats, Hawaiian wild pigs, wild sheep, mouflon, antelope, and black-tailed deer make up the big-game family in Hawaii. Axis deer, goats, and pigs support the bulk of the big-game hunting.

The major huntable populations of axis deer are on the islands of Molokai and Lanai where there are an estimated five thousand animals. Public hunting units 4, 5, 6, and 7 near the center of the long, narrow island are the major hunting areas on the Island of Molokai. Units 1 and 2 covering the northwestern third of Lanai are the major deer-lands on that small island.

Wild goats are found on all of the islands and they range from sea level to the summit of Haleakala on Maui. They, too, roam Units 1 and 2 of Lanai and Units 1, 2, 3, 4, 5, and 6, on the Island of Molokai. There are also good populations along the western coast of Kauai, in all hunting units on Maui, and there are special goat hunts on the Island of Hawaii.

Wild pigs, in a rich conglomeration of sizes and colors, though most are all black, live abundantly on the Islands of Kauai, Oahu, Molokai and Hawaii, and less abundantly on Maui. They live primarily in the wet forests, but also in semi deserts and ranch pasturelands.

Wild sheep and mouflon are found primarily on the "big island" of Hawaii, and to a lesser extent, mouflon are found on Lanai. Pronghorn antelope are now limited to the northern end of Lanai, and black-tailed deer live in small populations on the Island of Kauai.

Ring-necked pheasants are found in reasonable abundance on all of the islands. Japanese quail also inhabit all of the islands—but sparsely. Both lace-necked and barred doves also occur on all of the islands, the lace-necked from sea level to four thousand feet or more and the barred dove everywhere except in the dense rain forests. Pheasants live wherever there is suitable habitat—even at seven-thousand-foot elevations and in relatively heavy forest cover. Japanese quail are found primarily on pasturelands above seven thousand feet. Hot spots for the barred dove are the southwestern shore of Molokai, the Ewa District of Oahu, and Puako in Hawaii. Lace-necked doves are generally abundant.

Japanese blue pheasants are limited to the windward slopes of Mauna Kea and Mauna Loa on the Island of Hawaii. The Islands of Molokai and Hawaii also support the major California quail populations. Chukar partridge are found in huntable numbers on Hawaii, Maui, and Lanai. While wild pigeons are not hunted at the present, they occur on the Islands of Hawaii, Lanai, Oahu, and Molokai. The Barbary partridge is found on the Island of Hawaii only.

Black francolins inhabit all islands except Lanai and Oahu, and Erckel's francolins appear in appreciable numbers on Hawaii, Lanai, Oahu, and Kauai. Grey francolins are abundant on Lanai and are also found on other islands. Lanai is also the top island for Gambel's quail.

Rio Grande turkeys occupy all islands except Kahoolawe, and bamboo partridge are found on Maui only.

A Hawaiian hunting trip can be an unforgettable experience.

12 • IDAHO—Wild Country Hunting

Oddly-shaped Idaho, its narrow northern border brushing Canada, rugged and beautiful, is a hunter's dream. With elk roaming many of its forty-four counties, Idaho is considered by many hunters as a prime big-game state. It is. In addition to its fine elk hunting, there are both mule and white-tailed deer, mountain goats, mountain bighorn sheep, antelope, Shiras moose, an abundance of black bears, and fair populations of mountain lions. Merriam's wild turkeys furnish limited hunting.

Often overlooked is the fact that Idaho is a top bird-hunting state. For example, the state boasts five kinds of grouse and four species of quail. Quail include the bobwhite, Gambel's, mountain, and California. Almost forty percent of the state's 83,557 square miles are in forests, and the forest grouse include the ruffed, blue, and spruce. Sage and sharp-tailed grouse of the prairies round out the family. Other birds include pheasants, Hungarian partridge, chukar partridge, and mourning doves. The pheasant is the top game bird in Idaho, however.

While squirrels are protected, there is an abundance of rabbits—cottontails, pygmy rabbits, snowshoe hares, and jackrabbits.

The waterfowl hunting is excellent, with ducks, Canada geese, and a few snow geese furnishing most of the shooting.

Coyotes are plentiful in Idaho, and there are a few foxes, badgers, and raccoons. The high prices being paid for bobcat pelts are depleting their once abundant numbers. The Idaho Fish and Game Department is seeking protection for the little cats. Varmint hunters concentrate on ground squirrels, rockchucks, and jackrabbits.

With 73 percent of Idaho under public ownership, locating hunting land is no real problem.

There are fourteen national forests in Idaho, and together they furnish in excess of twenty million acres of public hunting land. Complete information and valuable maps can be had by writing the various forest headquarters at the address given for each forest. They are Boise at Boise, ID 83706; Cache at Montpelier, ID 83254; Caribou at Pocatello, ID 83201; Challis at Challis, ID 83226; Clearwater at Orofino, ID 83544; Idaho Panhandle at Coeur d'Alene, ID 83814; Nezperce at Grangeville, ID 83530; Payette at McCall, ID 83638; Salmon at Salmon, ID 83467; Sawtooth at 1525 Addison Avenue East, Twin Falls, ID 83301; Targhee at 420 North Bridge Street, St. Anthony, ID 83445; Bitterroot at Hamilton, MT 59840; Kootenai at Libby, MT 59923; and Lolo at Missoula, MT 59801.

The Curlew National Grasslands offers forty-seven thousand acres of bird and small-game hunting in the southeast near the Utah border. Maps and hunting details are available at the Caribou National Forest Headquarters at the address given above.

Idaho also has big chunks of Bureau of Land Management land in the southwestern part of the state, in the south central near Twin Falls, and in the southeastern near Pocatello. There are also smaller patches scattered about the state, mostly at the lower elevations. An excellent map, called *Idaho Recreation Map*, can be obtained by writing the Bureau of Land Management, Federal Building, Box 2237, Boise, Idaho 83701. This map shows the location of all public lands in the state.

While federal lands offer almost unlimited hunting opportunities, there is also a good deal of public land administered by various state agencies.

State forests in the vicinity of McCall, Priest Lake, and Orofino offer limited public hunting. The Idaho Game and Fish Department also administers a limited number of public hunting areas and wildlife-management areas. There are also approximately 150 public access areas open to hunting, though they were acquired primarily to provide access to larger chunks of hunting lands previously inaccessible to the public.

Included among the wildlife-management areas are Deer Flat, Fort Boise, and Sand Creek.

More complete information on the state forests, wildlife-management areas, and the public access areas can be obtained by writing the Idaho Fish and Game Department, 600 South Walnut Street, Box 25, Boise, Idaho 83707. The department can help in planning hunts to specific areas.

The mule-deer hunting is fine in Idaho. *Courtesy of Idaho Fish and Game Department.*

There is so much good public hunting land in Idaho that there is really little reason to hunt private land. However, the hunter must obtain permission from the landowner before entering his land to hunt. Shooting across public highways is prohibited.

The ring-necked pheasant is the top bird in a state noted for its varied bird hunting. Much of the best ringneck hunting is on private lands, but the Bureau of Land Management lands along the rivers offer good hunting. The Fort Boise Wildlife Management Area offers good pheasant hunting, and the best hunting for the gaudy bird is generally in the southern part of the state. Hungarian partridge are found in the same general range with the pheasant.

Chukar partridge hunting is good along the banks of the Boise, Payette, and Snake Rivers. This general area is also tops for quail, primarily California quail, though three other species occur in the state.

Forest grouse—ruffed, blue, and spruce—are likely to be found in any of the national forests, with the ruffed preferring the scrubby, tangled growth over the more mature forest favored by the blue and spruce.

The big sage-grouse harvest is fairly large in Idaho, with the prairie birds being most plentiful in the Upper Snake River region.

Mule deer are found throughout the state. Thanks to the vast national forests, finding good deer country is seldom a problem. One good area is the forest mountains south of Lewiston, but much of it is privately owned. The Salmon River near Challis is also good. The quality of the deer hunting varies from season to season, so it is wise to check with the Fish and Game Department before settling on an area. Most of the whitetails found in Idaho are north of the Salmon River.

The elk hunting is usually best in the Primitive Areas of the National Forests and the Lochsa, Selway, and Chamberlain Basin areas are usually dependable.

Sheep and goats, hunted by special permits only, are found mostly at the higher elevations of the Salmon River drainage, and black bears, reasonably abundant, are found throughout the forested regions of the state.

Finding a place to hunt in Idaho is rarely a problem, but settling on one of the rich variety of opportunities can be frustrating.

13 • ILLINOIS—For Cropland Hunting

Stretching almost 400 miles from north to south and covering 56,400 square miles, Illinois is a fringe plains state. Teeming with people, farms and industry, it also offers good hunting—mostly for those game species associated with an agricultural community.

For the average hunter, Illinois is tops for cottontail rabbits and squirrels. Both are abundant. Raccoons are plentiful, and coon hunting is a favorite sport. Both gray and red foxes provide good hunting for hound men. A thriving population of woodchucks rounds out the small-game hunting.

The white-tailed deer hunting is surprisingly good for a state so densely populated. Hunting is restricted to the bow and arrow, shotgun, and muzzle-loader.

Pheasants in the northern part of the state and quail in the west and south provide the cream of the game-bird hunting. The best hunting for both birds is found in the farmlands, where securing permission is not always easy, though far from impossible. There are a few Hungarian partridge in the extreme northwest, good dove populations, and scattered rails, snipes, and woodcocks. The wild turkey is making a comeback in the southern part of the state, as it is throughout much of America.

The Mississippi River has made Illinois famous as a waterfowl-hunting state, and the goose hunting is particularly good. Duck hunting is also much better than that in many parts of the Midwest. Private clubs and commercial shooting areas support much of the waterfowl hunting.

The Shawnee National Forest, in scattered blocks in the extreme southern tip of the state, provides 211,000 acres of prime hunting land, much of it along the Mississippi and Ohio Rivers. Maps and hunting information can be obtained by writing the Supervisor, Shawnee National Forest, Harrisburg, IL 62946. The U.S. Army Corps of Engineers is another major federal landowner in Illinois and has opened thousands of acres of prime bottomland along the Mississippi River for public hunting. Information on hunting this land can be obtained from the Illinois Department of Conservation, 605 State Office Building, 400 South Spring Street, Springfield, IL 62706.

There is limited public hunting on the Crab Orchard and Mark Twain National Wildlife Refuges, and the Spring Lake National Wildlife Refuge offers good bottomland hunting along the Mississippi River. Information on these public hunting areas is available from the Department of Conservation or from the Crab Orchard National Wildlife Refuge, P.O. Box J, Carterville, IL 62918.

Utilizing state parks, state forests, federal lands and refuges, and its own conservation areas and wildlife-management areas, the Department of Conservation provides public hunting on more than seventy hunting areas. Collectively, they provide hunting for every game species in the state, and range in size from 75-acre Bluff Lake Wildlife Management Area to 15,680-acre Carlyle Lake Wildlife Management Area. A list of these lands and the game available can be obtained from the Department of Conservation.

Still, private lands—clubs, farms, and commercial hunting lands —support the bulk of the hunting in crowded Illinois. Such lands often provide superb hunting for small game, waterfowl, and upland birds.

The law with respect to hunting on private land simply states the hunter must obtain the owner's permission before entering his lands. Shooting, hunting, or allowing dogs to hunt within two hundred yards of a dwelling without obtaining permission is prohibited.

Shooting preserves are numerous in Illinois, and they offer a wide variety of bird hunting. A list of these preserves can be obtained from the Department of Conservation. There are over seventy of them well-spaced throughout the state. Duck hunting clubs also offer good waterfowl hunting opportunities, either by membership or daily fees. A list of these clubs can be obtained from the Department of Conservation or from Tom McNally, Outdoor Editor, the *Chicago Tribune*, Chicago, Illinois.

Illinois has the largest wintering population of Canada geese in the Mississippi Flyway—over 400,000 birds in good seasons. The fine waterfowl hunting attracts a good deal of attention in the state. In addition to

Goose hunting is tops in the Mississippi River valley of Illinois. *Courtesy of Illinois Department of Conservation.*

the duck clubs, good hunting is available on the U. S. Corps of Engineers lands along the Mississippi River bottoms and various public hunting areas throughout the state. Blinds on state-owned or managed lands are allocated once every two years, but other hunters may use the blinds when they are not occupied by the licensee. The Department of Conservation can supply complete information on the availability of blinds.

In addition to the U.S. Army Corps of Engineers lands, good public waterfowl hunting areas include Anderson Lake Conservation Area, Baldwin River Bottoms Wildlife Management Area, Larue Swamp, Bend Lake, and Shelbyville Wildlife Management Areas, Calhoun County Federal Lands, Crab Orchard National Wildlife Refuge, and W. W. Powers Conservation Area. Carlyle Lake and Oakwood Bottoms Wildlife Management Areas are popular for walk-in hunting.

While croplands probably offer the best pheasant hunting, there is reasonably good hunting on many public hunting areas. Special areas on which permits are required include Carlyle Lake, Des Plaines, Chain O'

Lakes, and Green River, Iroquios County, and Richland County Conservation Areas. Other good general pheasant hunting areas include Big River State Forest, Fox Ridge State Park, and Marshall County Conservation Area.

Quail, like pheasants, prosper best in the croplands, but there is reasonably good hunting on Crawford County and Hamilton County Conservation Areas, Pyramid State Park, and Trail of Tears State Forest.

Doves may be found on many of the public hunting areas, including Iroquois County and Green River Conservation Areas and Red Hills State Park.

All of the timbered public hunting areas offer good squirrel hunting, but the best is probably along the timbered river bottoms of the Shawnee National Forest.

The Shawnee National Forest is also an excellent choice for deer and turkeys, though deer may also be found on other southern and western public hunting lands. Deer and turkey hunting are limited to residents or to nonresidents who own land in Illinois. Limited in number, five-dollar permits are distributed on the basis of an annual drawing.

Finally, rabbits, raccoons, and foxes range the state.

Hunting has not yet succumbed to progress in Illinois.

14 • INDIANA—For Small Game

With over five million people crowded into its 36,291 square miles, Indiana offers surprisingly good hunting. The bobwhite quail is the most important upland game bird, and the combined rabbit and squirrel bag tops two million annually and nudges the three-million mark in good years.

In addition to quail there are modest populations of pheasants, ruffed grouse, and Hungarian partridge for the bird hunter. Fair rail, snipe, and woodcock hunting complete the bird picture.

Cottontail rabbits are abundant, and both fox and gray squirrels abound in the woodlands. Foxes, raccoons, and opossums furnish fine sport for hound men and night hunters.

Indiana waterfowl hunting is not fabulous, but the numerous lakes, reservoirs, and streams provide fair hunting. Jump shooting along the rivers is popular.

The big-game hunter has fair populations of white-tailed deer and turkeys to satisfy his appetite, though the kill for neither species is large.

The Hoosier National Forest, 117,906 acres of public land in two sections in the south-central part of the state, is the major federal land in Indiana. The hunter can get maps and hunting information by writing the Forest Supervisor, Hoosier National Forest, Bedford, Indiana 47421. Also under the jurisdiction of the National Forest Supervisor is some additional land labeled Land Utilization Projects. It bears looking into. Other federal lands include the Crane U.S. Naval Ammunition Depot in Martin County, Camp Atterbury in Bartholomew County, and Jefferson Proving Ground in Jefferson and Ripley Counties. Hunting is permitted on these military lands, and details can be obtained from the Department of Natural Resources, State of Indiana, Room 612, State

Office Building, Indianapolis, Indiana 46204, but the hunter should contact the military officer in charge for hunting permission.

The Department of Natural Resources also owns or leases thirty tracts of public hunting land totaling thousands of acres. Called state fish-and-wildlife areas, they are scattered throughout Indiana, but the greatest concentrations are in the northern and southern thirds of the state. Central Indiana has very few public hunting lands.

In addition to the state fish-and-wildlife areas, there are a dozen state forests on which public hunting is permitted. These forest lands total well over 100,000 acres.

Full information on hunting these state-owned lands is available from the Department of Natural Resources. The department can also furnish information on hunting on the lands of the state-owned, flood-control reservoirs: There are seven in Indiana.

When writing the Department of Natural Resources, the hunter should ask for a copy of a map called Department of Natural Resources Property Guide. It shows the location by county of the state fish-and-wildlife areas, the state forests, and the flood-control reservoirs. These public lands are also shown on the official *Indiana Highway Map*, a copy of which is available from the Indiana State Highway Commission, Room 1201, 100 North Senate Avenue, Indianapolis, Indiana 46204.

While there is a fair amount of public hunting land in Indiana, the vast farmlands support the bulk of the hunting for just about all species of game. The Indiana posting law is a stiff one, however, and the hunter should proceed with caution when entering private lands. The law states it is illegal to fish, hunt, trap, or shoot with any kind of firearm upon any privately owned land without first securing the consent of the owner or tenant. The law goes even further by limiting the liability of the owner for injury sustained by people entering his premises for the purpose of hunting without first obtaining his permission.

Because of the heavy pressure and tremendous demands on hunting lands, many landowners reserve their hunting for themselves and their friends. Still, there is much hunting done on private lands. The Department of Natural Resources, through its Division of Fish and Game, encourages farmers to cooperate in permitting closely regulated public hunting. There is also some fee hunting in the state.

The abundant rabbit populations furnish an annual harvest of just under a million animals, and the bulk of the kill is made on private lands. The cottontail thrives best on farmlands. Still, there are rabbits on just about all of the public lands mentioned above. Good public hunting lands include the Atterbury, Pigeon River, and Tri-County Fish and Wildlife Areas.

The annual squirrel harvest in Indiana is high. *Indiana Division of Fish and Wildlife Photo.*

Indiana's abundant fox squirrel populations thrive best in the farmlands and along the stream bottoms, with the equally abundant gray found mostly in the forests. Just about any public hunting tract with a modest supply of hardwoods should furnish squirrel hunting. The big Hoosier National Forest is good, for grays particularly. The state forests rate fair to excellent, with most of them at least good. Good state fish-and-wildlife areas include Atterbury, Brush Creek, Glendale, Jasper-Pulaski, and Springs Valley.

The annual quail harvest approaches three-quarters of a million birds, and the bobwhite is by far the top game bird in Indiana. The best hunting is found in the southern half of the state and on private lands, though there are a few birds scattered throughout Indiana. Good public-hunting lands include the Willow Slough and Winamac Fish and Wildlife Areas, and big 5180-acre Greene-Sullivan State Forest in Greene and Sullivan Counties.

Most of the modest pheasant populations are found in the northern half of the state, and the major range of the Hungarian partridge is in the east-central part of Indiana. The Hoosier National Forest is a good bet for ruffed grouse.

A major portion of the white-tailed-deer kill comes from the military areas—Crane U. S. Naval Ammunition Depot, Camp Atterbury, and Jefferson Proving Grounds. The Hoosier National Forest also offers fair deer hunting.

Turkey hunting in most years is limited to the spring gobbler season, with the hunting fair in the Hoosier National Forest and in several state forests, including Clark, Jackson-Washington, and Pike.

While Indiana is not a major waterfowl state, fair hunting can be enjoyed by those willing to work for it. Hovey Lake Fish and Wildlife Area is one of the better public hunting areas, but many of the small streams in the southern part of the state offer good jump shooting.

Indiana is a good example of a state offering good hunting in the face of an exploding human population making ever-increasing demands on land and water resources.

15 • IOWA—New Pheasant Capital

With an estimated annual harvest of an excess of one and one-half million birds, Iowa has a just claim on the current title of Pheasant Capital of the United States. It now leads all other states in the production of these gaudy birds.

The big plains state has an area of 56,290 square miles and a population of almost three million people.

When compared to many other states, Iowa has limited public hunting lands, but federal, state, and county lands total approximately 275,000 acres.

There are no national forests in Iowa and very little federal land. The DeSota National Wildlife Refuge on the Missouri River provides late-season waterfowling. There is also excellent waterfowling on private lands in the vicinity of 2,077-acre Union Slough National Wildlife Refuge in north-central Iowa, but the refuge itself is not usually open to hunting. Write the Iowa Conservation Commission, 300 Fourth Street, Des Moines, Iowa 50319, for hunting information.

The great majority of the public hunting lands in Iowa are in the form of the Iowa Public Hunting Areas. There are approximately 250 of them, and they provide over 250,000 acres of prime public hunting land at convenient locations throughout the state. Some are small, such as 22-acre Decatur Bend in Monona County and 24-acre Perkins Marsh in Palo Alto County, but there are also some sizeable ones—25,542-acre Red Rock Area, 14,000-acre Hawkeye Wildlife Area, and 13,730-acre Rathbun Wildlife Area. These areas are described in detail in a colorful publication, Iowa Hunting Guide, available for twenty-five cents from the Conservation Commission.

Another excellent public hunting area is the Upper Mississippi River Fish and Wildlife Refuge on the eastern border. A portion of it is open to hunting. Write the Conservation Commission for information.

Also unique to Iowa are the approximately eight thousand acres of land in county hunting areas. These are administered by County Conservation Boards and are used mostly by county residents, though they are open to public hunting generally. The Conservation Commission can supply additional information on these public hunting lands.

In spite of the strides being made by the Conservation Commission and county boards to secure public hunting lands, the vast private lands of the state offer the best hunting. A courteous request will bring permission to hunt many rich Iowa farmlands.

The gaudy ring-necked pheasant gets top billing in Iowa, with the state offering possibly the best pheasant hunting in America. Surprisingly, the state is also a top bobwhite quail state, though this normally southern bird takes a decided back seat to the pheasant. Ruffed grouse, Hungarian partridge, rails, snipes, and woodcocks round out the game-bird populations.

A fair white-tailed deer herd and introduced turkeys are the big-game offerings in Iowa. Both deer and turkeys are limited to resident hunters only.

Both fox and gray squirrels, cottontails, and jackrabbits are the major targets of the small-game hunter. Raccoons and foxes abound, and night hunting is popular and productive of coons. Coyotes are unprotected, but woodchucks are on the game-animal list.

Waterfowl hunting is excellent in the state, particularly along the Mississippi and Missouri River Valleys. The goose hunting rates with the best in the nation.

Pheasants occur generally statewide, but the best hunting is found in the east-central and southwestern part of the state. Good public hunting areas include Meadow Lake, Walters Creek, Rathbun Wildlife Area, Dudgeon Lake, Sweet Marsh, Big Marsh, Ventura Marsh, Trumbull Lake, East Okoboji, Spirit Lake, Riverton Area, Elk Grove Wildlife Area, Red Rock Area, Loess Hills, Otter Creek Marsh, Rice Lake, and Elk Creek.

The primary quail range is in the southern part of the state, with the best close to the border. Good public hunting areas include Adair County Wildlife Area, Walters Creek Area, Rathbun Wildlife Area, Stephens Forest, Eldon Game Area, Elk Grove Wildlife Area, South River Access, Shimek Forest, Red Rock Area, Loess Hills, and Weise Slough. Many of the better quail areas are also pheasant areas, providing opportunities for mixed bags.

The pheasant harvest in Iowa approaches two million birds. *Iowa Conservation Commission Photo.*

The best grouse hunting is in the wooded hill country of the northeastern part of Iowa. French Creek, Lansing Wildlife, Yellow Forest, Sny McGill-Red Cedar Access, and Volga River Public Hunting Areas offer limited grouse hunting. They also offer woodcock hunting.

The best deer hunting is found in the southern, western, and northeastern regions of Iowa. Numerous public hunting areas offer whitetail hunting. The larger ones include Yellow River Forest, Rathbun Wildlife Area, Elk Grove Wildlife Area, Green Island, Hawkeye Wildlife Area, Shimek Forest, Lake Odessa, Muscatine Slough, Stephens Forest, Red Rock Area, Loess Hills, Otter Creek Marsh, Brushy Creek, and Elk Creek Marsh.

The turkey hunting is much more limited. It is found only in Shemik Forest and Stephens Forest Public Hunting Areas.

Squirrels abound in the forested river bottoms and woodlots of Iowa on both private land and in the public hunting areas. Finding a place to hunt squirrels is rarely a problem, though the southern half of the state has most abundant populations. The gray squirrel prefers the vast forest areas, while the fox squirrel likes the park-like farm woodlots. Bunny-busters bag well over two million cottontail rabbits a year in

Iowa, and they are found just about statewide, though the southern portion of the state is best. Jackrabbits are most abundant in the western regions.

Raccoons are plentiful all over Iowa, particularly along the wooded river bottoms. Most of the public hunting areas offer some coon hunting, though the forested ones are by far the best. The fox is found statewide, and coyotes occur mostly along the Missouri River.

The state's fine waterfowling is best along the Mississippi and Missouri Rivers. Farm ponds and small marshes also offer good hunting. Good public hunting areas include Lansing Big Lake, Sweet Marsh, Clear Lake, Barringer Slough, East Okoboji, Spirit Lake, and Lake Odessa. Hunting is also good in the northern, natural, lakes country. The southern regions offer excellent late-season waterfowling.

Excellent pheasant and waterfowl hunting and small game are the hunting story in Iowa.

16 • KANSAS—A Game-Bird State

To many eastern hunters, Kansas is just a long drive across the plains en route to hunting in Colorado and other western states. It is an interesting trip—four hundred miles east to west. The highways are excellent and a joy to travel, but the big plains country tends to get monotonous after a couple of hundred miles.

Unfortunately, very few hunters realize they are passing through some of the finest bird hunting in America. The pheasant, though declining in numbers at the present, is the state's top game bird, but the bobwhite quail is challenging the ringneck for the number one game-bird spot. There are scaled quail in the southwest, and the Flint Hills of eastern Kansas contain the largest single concentration of greater prairie chickens in the United States. The mourning-dove hunting is also excellent.

Kansas waterfowlers enjoy good duck and goose hunting, and there is fair hunting for woodcocks, snipes, and rails.

Deer herds are holding steady, with muleys in the west and whitetails in the east. Antelope are also making a comeback, with limited hunting now permitted in the northwest part of the state. The wild turkey is joining the deer and antelope to bring back big-game hunting, at the present limited to residents.

Squirrel hunting is good but spotty, and cottontail rabbits are found all over the state. Jackrabbits are abundant in the west.

Coyotes, bobcats, foxes, and raccoons attract some hunting attention, and there are prairie dogs and woodchucks for the varmint hunter.

It is the fine game-bird hunting, however, that draws most of the out-of-staters to Kansas.

With a population of two and one-half million people and an area of 82,264 square miles, Kansas is not crowded, and there is plenty of hunting room.

Federal lands in Kansas are limited, but the Cimarron National Grasslands offers 106,000 acres of prime hunting land in the southwestern corner of the state. Maps and hunting information can be obtained from the Resident Manager, U.S. Forest Service, Elkhart, Kansas 67950.

Lands adjacent to the various U.S. Army Corps of Engineers Reservoirs provide another 22,600 acres of public hunting land. Information can be obtained by writing the Resident Manager at Strawn, KS 66839, for John Redmond Reservoir; at Marquette, KS 67464, for Kanopolis Reservoir; at Olivet, KS 66519, for Melvern Reservoir; and at Vassar, KS 66543, for Pomona Reservoir. Most of the Corps of Engineers offices are located at the dam sites.

The Flint Hills National Wildlife Refuge is located on the John Redmond Reservoir lands, and hunting information can be obtained from the Resident Manager at Burlington, Kansas 66839. The Quivira National Wildlife Refuge offers 7,990 acres of public hunting in the south-central part of Kansas. Maps and information are available from the Resident Manager, Stafford, Kansas 67578. Both of these refuges are under the jurisdiction of the U.S Fish and Wildlife Service.

The U.S. Bureau of Reclamation owns 2,290 acres of public hunting land adjacent to its Kirwin Reservoir in the northern part of the state. Information can be obtained by writing the Resident Manager at Kirwin, Kansas 67644. Hunting is under the jurisdiction of the U.S. Fish and Wildlife Service.

While the Federal lands offer many hunting opportunities, it is the familiar "Kansas Forestry, Fish and Game Commission" sign with yellow background and black lettering that signals the heart of public hunting in the big plains state. This sign is used to mark a game-management area owned or licensed by the Commission. There are forty-eight such areas scattered throughout the state, and the commission is adding others as land and funds become available. Collectively, they provide almost 300,000 acres of public hunting land, some of it the very best in Kansas.

Some of the game-management areas are small. The Almenia Diversion Game Management Area is only eleven acres, but most are several hundred acres at the minimum, and many contain thousands of acres. Glen Elder Game Management Area near Cawker City has 25,100 acres of hunting land. Other big ones include Cedar Bluff, Cheyenne Bot-

Kansas hunters Lawrence and Thayne Smith admire a bag of scaled quail. *Bob Gooch Photo.*

toms, Elk City, Fall River, Milford, Perry, and Tuttle Creek.

Cheyenne Bottoms, Hain Lake, Jamestown, Marais des Cygnes, and Neesho are primarily waterfowl-management areas.

A handy little folder that describes these forty-eight game-management areas and locates them by verbal description and by map can be obtained by writing the Kansas Forestry, Fish and Game Commission, Box 1028, Pratt, Kansas 67124.

Kansas is primarily an agricultural state with 95 percent of its land under private ownership. Some of the very best hunting in the state is found in the rich farmlands. Since hunting pressure is relatively light in Kansas, with very little pressure from nonresident hunters, permission to hunt private land is not too difficult to get.

Although title to all game is vested in the people of Kansas, it is illegal to enter the land of a farmer or other landowner without first obtaining his permission. This protection for the landowner extends to public roads adjacent to his property and to railroad rights-of-way through his property. It is illegal to hunt from roads or railroads without first obtaining the permission of the adjacent landowner.

The ring-necked pheasant, the bobwhite quail's rival as the number one game bird in Kansas, is found primarily in the western part of the state. Pheasants occur in fair numbers all over the state, however, with the exception of the southeast, where they occur but are scarce. Good public hunting areas include Kirwin Reservoir, Norton, Sheridan, Glen Elder, and Cedar Bluff Game Management Areas and Cimarron National Grasslands.

The best quail hunting is found in the eastern part of the state and mostly on private lands where farm crops favor the bobwhite. Fortunately for the quail hunter, however, there are a number of public hunting areas in the prime bobwhite range. Included are big Milford and Tuttle Creek Game Management Areas. The Cimarron National Grasslands offers good public hunting for scaled quail, or blue quail as the scaled quail is often called.

The Flint Hills National Wildlife Refuge is a good bet for prairie chickens, but the best hunting is found on private lands in the east-central part of Kansas.

The bird hunter will enjoy Kansas.

17 • KENTUCKY—Birds and Small Game

Kentucky's four million people live in forty thousand square miles, and many of them enjoy some of the finest small-game hunting in the Nation.

In the land of Daniel Boone and the Kentucky rifle, it is appropriate that the squirrel should be the number one game animal. It is. Kentucky hunters bag over a million annually, most of them grays, but there is also good fox-squirrel hunting along the river bottoms. Cottontail rabbits are also popular, but are on the decline because of changes in land use.

The bobwhite quail and the mourning dove fly neck and neck for the number one game bird in Kentucky. Most authorities give their vote to the quail, but anyone who has participated in an invitational dove shoot on one of the famous Kentucky plantations would question this.

In addition to the dove and quail, there are a few ruffed grouse, woodcocks, turkeys, rails and snipes. The small-game hunter will find both red and gray foxes, raccoons, opossum, and woodchucks, in addition to rabbits and squirrels.

While Kentucky is not noted for its big-game hunting, there is fair white-tailed deer hunting in parts of the state. The black bear, near extinction, is fully protected.

While waterfowl hunting is mediocre at best, there is fair goose shooting and scattered hunting for ducks.

The Daniel Boone National Forest and the Jefferson National Forest are the major federal lands in Kentucky, though there are various military lands, Atomic Energy lands, U.S. Army Corps of Engineers lands, and lands of the Tennessee Valley Authority.

Maps and hunting information on the Daniel Boone National Forest are available from the Supervisor, Daniel Boone National Forest, Box 727, Winchester, Kentucky 40391. This national forest provides 630,000 acres of public land. Approximately 960 acres of the Jefferson National Forest penetrate the state from neighboring Virginia. The Forest Supervisor is located in the Poff Federal Building, 3517 Brandon Avenue, S.W., Roanoke, Virginia 24018.

Generally, the best source of information on the military, Atomic Energy lands, the U. S. Army Corps of Engineer lands, and the lands of the Tennessee Valley Authority is the Kentucky Department of Fish and Wildlife Resources, Capital Plaza, Frankfort, KY 40601. However, information on the Tennessee Valley Authority Land Between the Lakes area can be obtained from Land Between the Lakes, Golden Pond, KY 42231. The Department of the Army Corps, of Engineers, P.O. Box 2127, Huntington, WV 25721, can furnish information on Dewey and Fishtrap Reservoirs.

Kentucky's forty-five public hunting areas, though on the lands of various agencies of the state and federal governments, are under the jurisdiction of the Department of Fish and Wildlife Resources for management and the regulation of hunting. These areas are the very heart of public hunting in Kentucky. A handy brochure called Places to Hunt can be obtained from the department. It locates and describes each area and contains a good reference map.

The best hunting in Kentucky is usually found on private lands, particularly for doves, quail, and small game. In Kentucky, however, it is illegal to enter private lands to hunt without first obtaining the permission of the owner. Many Kentucky landowners will grant this permission.

The Daniel Boone National Forest is an ideal place to hunt squirrels, the top game species in the state. The Land Between the Lakes area is also good. Many of the public hunting areas offer good squirrel hunting. Among them are Beech Creek, Dale Hollow, Kentucky Ridge State Forest, Stearns, Fort Knox, Twin Eagle, Fort Campbell, West Kentucky, and Reelfoot Lake.

The bobwhite quail, generally considered the top game bird in the state, is found statewide, but the best hunting is in western and west-central Kentucky. The better hunting is on private farmlands, but there is some quail hunting on the public hunting areas. The better ones include Fort Campbell, Higginson-Henry, Kentucky Lake, Lake Cumberland, Green River, Fort Knox, Dewey Lake, and Beech Creek.

Doves, extremely popular among Kentucky hunters, are most abundant in the agricultural areas of central and western Kentucky. In-

The dove presses the bobwhite quail as the number one game bird in Kentucky. *Bob Gooch Photo.*

vitational dove shoots are popular here, and they take on the atmosphere of social events as hunters gather for refreshments when they fill their limits in the bird-rich fields. Good public hunting areas include Central Kentucky, Curtis Gates Lloyd, Fort Knox, Green River, Lake Cumberland, Mullins, Twin Eagle, Ballard County, Higginson-Henry,

Kentucky Lake, Land Between the Lakes, and West Kentucky.

Though found all over Kentucky, rabbits are most abundant in the Bluegrass Region and in the western part of the state. There are a few swamp rabbits along the Mississippi River bottoms. Good public hunting areas include Beech Creek, Dale Hollow, Daniel Boone National Forest, Dewey Lake, Kentenia State Forest, Barren Lake, Curtis Gates Llody, Fort Knox, Green River, Mullins, Rough River, Fort Campbell, Jones-Keeney, Kentucky Lake, Peal, Sloughs, and West Kentucky.

Good game management has brought the ruffed-grouse populations to the point where today the hardy mountain birds afford good shooting in the extreme eastern part of Kentucky. The Daniel Boone National Forest provides good hunting, and the better public hunting areas include Buckhorn Lake, Crank's Creek, Dewey Lake, Fishtrap Lake, Kentenia State Forest, Kentucky Ridge State Forest, Mead Forest, Olympia State Forest, Stearns, and Tygarts State Forest.

The best deer-hunting areas are the two large military reservations, Fort Knox and Fort Campbell. The public hunting areas in the far western part of the state also offer good hunting.

Limited and carefully regulated turkey hunting is permitted on the Land Between the Lakes area.

The Ballard County public hunting area is the top waterfowling area in Kentucky, but scattered lakes, rivers, and reservoirs add duck hunting—and round out a rich variety of Kentucky hunting.

18 • LOUISIANA—Sportsman's Paradise

Louisiana's 48,523 square miles of marshes, pine-covered hills, and delta bottomlands make this state on the Gulf of Mexico truly a sportsman's paradise, as the state's automobile tags proclaim. With an estimated five million acres of tidal marshes and 7,500 square miles of the state actually under water, Louisiana is indeed a unique hunting state unmatched anywhere else in America.

In the Kisatchie National Forest alone there are 150,000 acres of Federal land under game management programs, with another 445,301 acres open to public hunting, though not managed so intensively. Headquarters, where maps and general hunting information can be obtained, are located at 2500 Shreveport Highway, Pineville, Louisiana 71360. In addition to the national forest lands, the U.S. Fish and Wildlife Service has another 173,842 acres of federal refuge lands open to public hunting—mostly for waterfowl—but also offering limited hunting for other species. Complete information on hunting these rich, well-managed refuges can be obtained from the U.S. Fish and Wildlife Service, Sabine National Wildlife Refuge. MRH Box 107, Sulphur, Louisiana 70663.

The very heart of public hunting in Louisiana, however, is the 1,092,236 acres of wildlife-management areas set aside by the Louisiana Wildlife and Fisheries Commission. The commission owns outright 240,853 acres of these lands and leases another 707,262 acres from corporations, other government agencies, and individuals. Complete information is available from the Louisiana Department of Wildlife and Fisheries, 400 Royal Street, New Orleans, Louisiana 70130.

Collectively, they offer hunting for just about every game species found in the state. The various Louisiana waterways are the roadways to some of the best hunting not only for waterfowl but for other game as well. To open these waterways, the Department of Wildlife and Fisheries has been building boat ramps and parking areas throughout the state. A list of the ramps can be obtained by writing the Department at the above address.

There is also some good public hunting in the Atchafalaya Basin Floodway, but before entering this rich land of water and marshes, regulations should be requested from the Mississippi River Commission, U.S. Army Corps of Engineers, New Orleans, Louisiana 70113. For information on hunting the Toledo Bend Area, write Toledo Bend Map and Information, Sabine River Authority, P.O. Box 154-L, Anacoco, Louisiana 71403.

In addition to the state and federal lands, there are millions of acres of prime Louisiana hunting land owned by large timber-holding corporations. Much of this land is open to public hunting. Information on the corporate land is available from the Department of Wildlife and Fisheries.

As is the case in many eastern and southern states, the best hunting is often found on private lands—particularly for the farm species such as doves, quail, and rabbits. The posting law which governs access to private land varies to a degree between parishes, but basically it requires the owner to post signs conspicuously on land where he wants to prohibit hunting. The signs must be of adequate size and in clear view on fences or other boundaries. Additionally, the notice of posting must be published in the parish's official journal for several consecutive issues.

The white-tailed deer is Louisiana's most popular big-game animal, and the state has an abundance of deer scattered pretty much throughout the state. The greatest concentrations, however, are found in the hardwood deltas of the Mississippi and Atchafalaya Rivers. Good wildlife-management areas include Bodcau, Bohemia, Caney, Catahoula, Cities Service, Concordia, Jackson-Bienville, Red River, Saline, Thistlethwaite, Three Rivers, and Union. The annual deer harvest runs well in excess of eighty thousand animals.

An estimated population of ten thousands birds provides turkey hunting in forty-one of the state's parishes. The best turkey populations are found in the Florida parishes and in the northeast along the Mississippi River. The current turkey harvest is less than one thousand birds, but the flocks are expanding under careful management.

The black bear rounds out the big-game hunting in Louisiana, but the season is brief, running for a week in October.

Waterfowl hunting is a way of life in Louisiana. *Photo by Bob Dennie.*

Fox and gray squirrels, cottontails and swamp rabbits comprise the small-game hunting in Louisiana. The fox and gray squirrels and various subspecies provide excellent squirrel hunting throughout the state. The bayou gray is found along the Atchafalaya River, along the lower Mississippi River, and in the bayous of south Louisiana. The Bachman's fox squirrel is found east of the Mississippi, the delta fox squirrel along the Mississippi, Tensas, Ouachita, Atchafalaya, and Red River bottoms, and the big-headed fox squirrel in the uplands of the west. Both cottontails and swamp rabbits occur in an abundance throughout the state, the cottontail preferring the agricultural areas and the marshes, swamps, and bottomlands.

The bobwhite quail is the number one game bird in Louisiana. While the popular bobwhite is found throughout the state, the highest concentrations of birds are now found in the cutover pine woods in the southeast. There the public-spirited policies of the big timber companies offer excellent chances for quail hunting.

Three species of doves, the mourning dove, ground dove, and white-winged, occur in Louisiana. The mourning dove offers fast shooting in

the agricultural areas. Good wildlife-management areas include Bodcau, Cities Service, Fort Polk, Georgia-Pacific, Lutcher-Moore, Peason
Ridge, Union, and Wisner.

With over 75 percent of the migrant population wintering in the state,
Louisiana is a top woodcock state. The long-billed birds are found
throughout the state, but the Atchafalaya Basin is extremely productive
and popular.

Snipes and rails round out the game-bird list.

The most important wintering area for waterfowl east of the Rocky
Mountains, Louisiana offers some truly superb hunting for ducks and
geese. An estimated 75 to 80 percent of the hunting is concentrated in
the coastal marshes and rice fields of southern Louisiana, but Catahoula
Lake in central Louisiana is also an important wintering area for ducks.
White-fronted, blue, and snow geese make up the goose populations. In
addition to the vast federal refuge lands mentioned in the opening
paragraphs, the Department of Wildlife and Fisheries manages many
wildlife-management areas for ducks and geese. Both the federal and
state areas can be obtained from the addresses given previously. Notable
are the Pass-a-Loutre Waterfowl Management Area and the Sabine National Wildlife Refuge.

Hunting in Louisiana can be truly great.

19 • MAINE—North Woods Hunting

Outsized white-tailed deer and a healthy black bear population are the attractions that draw most out-of-state hunters to Maine. The state's one million people live in a land of thirty-three thousand square miles, but much of the northern part of the state is heavily forested, remote, and accessible only by scattered logging roads.

Prime white-tailed-deer and bear hunting are the big-game picture in Maine. Maine deer grow big. Many hunters wear shoulder patches attesting to membership in the Biggest Bucks in Maine Club. The hunter who bags a two-hundred-pound, field-dressed buck gains membership to the club. Moose are on the increase, but there is no open season on them.

Small-game hunting, also tops, includes both snowshoe rabbits and cottontails, gray squirrels, raccoons, bobcats, coyotes, and woodchucks. Lynx are protected.

The bird hunter will find an abundance of ruffed grouse, the king of the state's game birds, ring-necked pheasants, woodcocks, snipes, and rails.

The waterfowl hunting in Maine is rated fair to good, with the best along the coast. There is also a fair amount of shooting inland along the streams and on the numerous lakes, ponds, marshes, and beaver flowages.

While Maine has very little public land, there are seventeen million acres of private land available for public hunting. Much of this is in commercial forests owned by approximately a dozen major paper companies. It is prime hunting land. Over 95 percent of Maine's rich forests are under private ownership.

Federal lands are extremely limited in Maine, but seventy-seven thousand acres of the White Mountain National Forest extend into the western part of the state from New Hampshire. Headquarters for the National Forest is at Laconia, New Hampshire 03246. Write there for maps and hunting details.

State-owned lands are also limited, but the Maine Department of Inland Fisheries and Wildlife has been purchasing land for Wildlife Management Areas as funds become available. At the present there are nineteen of these areas totaling more than thirty thousand acres. The Department also retains flowage rights to three areas totaling nine thousand acres, leases or holds cooperative agreements to twenty-eight small tion between the landowners and Maine government agencies, such as permitted on most of these areas. Write the Maine Department of Inland Fisheries and Wildlife, 284 State Street, Augusta, Maine 04333, for details.

The hunter must therefore look to the vast private lands in Maine, and this is the route most hunters go. Landowners may forbid trespass either orally or by posting, however, and those who ignore these warnings are guilty of trespass and subject to stiff fines. While landowners are generally liberal with hunters, the hunter should have a clear understanding with the landowner before entering his land. North Maine Woods, two and one-half million acres of prime hunting land that includes both the Allagash and St. John Rivers, is a good example of privately owned land made available for hunting through close cooperation between the landowners and Maine government agencies such as the Bureau of Forestry, Bureau of Parks and Recreation, and the Department of Inland Fisheries and Wildlife. This prime hunting land is owned by thirteen private companies or estates and the state of Maine. Maps and hunting information can be obtained by writing the North Maine Woods, General Delivery, Presque Isle, Maine 04760.

There are many other companies, in northern Maine particularly, that open their lands to hunters under various arrangements. American Forest Products Industries, 1835 K Street, N.W., Washington, D.C. 20006, can provide information on most of them. The Paper Industry Information Office, 133 State Street, Augusta, Maine 04330, can also help. Major companies include the St. Regis Paper Company, 150 East 42nd Street, New York, NY 10017; International Paper Company, 220 East 42nd Street, New York, NY 10017; the Dead River Company, 55 Broadway, Bangor, ME 04401; and the Georgia Pacific Corporation, Woodland, ME 04694.

The white-tailed deer, the choice of most hunters who visit Maine, is

White-tailed deer grow big in Maine. *Courtesy of Maine Fish and Game Department.*

found all over the state, and the hunting is generally good statewide. The southern half of the state usually turns up the heaviest harvest, though hunting is also good in the less accessible northern wilderness areas. High-kill counties include Aroostook, Franklin, Hancock, Oxford, Penobscot, Piscataquis, Waldo, Washington, and York.

Maine's best bear country includes the counties of Aroostook, Franklin, Oxford, Piscataquis, Penobscot, and Somerset. Except in the southern coastal counties, the black bear is widely distributed in Maine, but the counties listed offer the best services in the way of accommodations and guides for bear hunters. They are also prime hunting counties.

Based on the total harvest, the ruffed grouse, or partridge as it is called in Maine, and the snowshoe hare run neck and neck. Grouse are found just about all over the state, but almost half of the kill comes from the west and southwest. Aroostook County is also good. Knowledgeable grouse hunters walk the logging roads and trails and hunt the cutovers and burns where new growth and scrub brush provide good cover.

Maine, with a good nesting population and heavy migration flights, is an excellent woodcock-state. Most of the kill comes from the southern half of the state, primarily because it is the hardest hunted. The area along the Canadian border is good. So are Franklin, Oxford, Penobscot, and Somerset Counties.

The snowshoe rabbit or hare is the prime small-game animal in Maine and is found in suitable habitat—alder swamps and evergreen forests—just about all over the state. Much of the kill comes from the southern half of the state, but only because the hunting is more concentrated in this more accessible part of Maine. Cottontails, not nearly so abundant, are found primarily along the coast and in the southern part of the state.

Merrymeeting Bay is famous for its excellent duck hunting, and there is good waterfowling all along the southern coast. Inland, the rivers and lakes offer fair shooting. A strip of Aroostook County along the New Brunswick border is good. The area between Rumford and Bangor in the southwest is also good for waterfowling. Snipe hunting in the marshes is good, but it attracts little attention.

There is good hunting down east.

20 • MARYLAND—Small Game and Waterfowl

Geographically diversified, Maryland's 10,577 square miles offer an amazing variety of hunting for a densely populated eastern state. Almost four and one-half million people live in this Middle Atlantic state.

White-tailed deer and wild turkeys are the big-game offering. The state's estimated seventy-five thousand deer are spread from the rugged Alleghenies to the flat coastal plains of the famous Eastern Shore. Under good management, the turkey flocks are on the increase.

The game bird offering is rich, including ring-necked pheasants, ruffed grouse, bobwhite quail, mourning doves, woodcocks, rails, and snipes.

The waterfowl hunter will find some of the best goose shooting in America on the agriculturally rich Eastern Shore. Black ducks, mallards, and other Atlantic Flyway ducks provide excellent waterfowling in Maryland's varied coastal waters and along the inland streams.

The small-game hunter will find an abundance of gray squirrels, a few fox squirrels which are protected, and little red squirrels in the western coniferous forests. The cottontail hunting is good, and there are some snowshoe hares in the western mountains. Both raccoons and opossums keep the night hunters happy.

The varmint hunter will find an abundance of woodchucks.

Public hunting lands in Maryland are not extensive, but 201, 921 acres of varied lands are so designated.

Federal lands in Maryland are extremely limited when compared to those in neighboring states. The Assateague Island National Seashore on the coast and the Catoctin National Park in the West are closed to

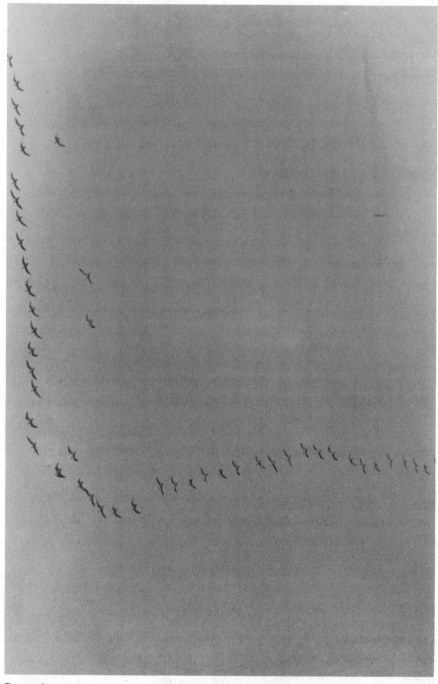

Goose hunting on the Eastern Shore of Maryland is nationally known. *Bob Gooch Photo.*

hunting. There is limited hunting on the Blackwater National Wildlife Refuge near Cambridge, but the area is not open every season. There are also special deer hunts on the Eastern Neck National Wildlife Refuge at Rock Hall, and white-tailed and sika deer hunting on Chincoteague National Wildlife Refuge on Assateague Island. Most of this refuge is in Virginia, but the northern tip extends into Maryland. Information on hunting these federal lands can be obtained from the General Services Administration, Federal Information Center, 31 Hopkins Plaza, Baltimore, Maryland 21201.

State-owned or leased lands support the bulk of the public hunting in Maryland. Most are under the administration of the Maryland Wildlife Administration, but the Maryland Forest and Park Services also opens some of its lands to public hunting.

The wildlife-management areas, providing most of the public hunting, stretch from east to west and from north to south, tapping just about every kind of hunting in the state. In the eastern region, there are areas ranging in size from 25-acre Sinepuxent Bay Wildlife Management Area to 12,749-acre Fishing Bay Wildlife Management Area. Sizeable ones include Pocomoke Sound, Cedar Island, Fairmont, Deal Island, and Ernest A. Vaughn. Also included in this region are 11,400-acre Pocomoke State Forest and 11,110-acre Wicomico State Forest. Write the Maryland Wildlife Administration, Eastern Regional Service Center, 920 Cooper Street, Salisbury, Maryland 21801, for information.

The central region includes 4,500-acre Whitaker Lands, 2,400-acre C and D Lands, 2,742-acre Elk Neck State Forest, and 2,619-acre Millington Wildlife Management Area, all administered by the Maryland Wildlife Administration, Central Regional Service Center, 103 North Main Street, Bel Air, Maryland 21014. Write there for information.

The Maryland Wildlife Administration, Southern Regional Service Center, Twenty-nine C Street, Laurel, Maryland 20810, can provide information on the McKee-Beshers, Hugg-Thomas, Myrtle Grove, and Merkle Wildlife Management Areas, and on the Cedarville and Doncaster State Forests.

Wildlife-management areas in the big western region range in size from 708-acre Billmeyer to 8,047-acre Dans Mountain in Allegany County. Also included in this region are Swallow Falls, Potomac, 52,690-acre Savage River, Green Ridge State Forests, and Deep Creek and Cunningham Falls State Parks. Write the Maryland Wildlife Administration, Western Regional Service Center, Highland Estate Naves Crossroads, Cumberland, Maryland 21502.

Limited hunting is permitted on the Hanover, Pretty Boy, and

Liberty Watersheds. Write the Maryland Wildlife Administration, Tawes State Office Building B-2, Annapolis, Maryland 21401.

The hunter needs the written permission of the owner to hunt private lands in Harford, Charles, Kent, Queen Annes, Caroline, and Talbot Counties, and written permission to hunt deer in Baltimore, Wicomico, Somerset and Howard Counties.

A Cooperative Wildlife Management Area Program has opened approximately five thousand acres of private land in Baltimore and Carroll Counties to public hunting.

All of the western wildlife-management areas offer deer hunting, and all except Cunningham Falls State Park offer turkeys. In the southern region all except Hugg-Thomas offer deer, but no turkeys. All four areas in the central region offer deer hunting, and in the eastern region, all except Cedar Island, Deal Island, Foster Estate, and Sinepuxent Bay offer deer hunting. Turkeys are generally limited to the western part of the state.

Grouse, like turkeys, are limited to the wildlife-management areas in the western region. Northern Maryland is the southernmost range of the ring-necked pheasant, but there is little or no public hunting land providing good pheasant hunting. Southern Maryland and the Eastern Shore are both famous for their fine quail hunting. The best is on private lands, but most of the eastern wildlife-management areas, with exception of the marsh areas managed for waterfowl, provide good hunting.

Doves, too, are most abundant on private lands, but the McKee-Beshers, Idylwild, Fishing Bay, and Ernest A. Vaughn Wildlife Management Areas offer dove hunting.

Woodcocks are found on Mt. Nebo, Dans Mountain, and Idylwild Wildlife Management Areas.

Squirrels are found on all of the wildlife-management areas in the western, central, and southern regions, and in most of those in the east except for the coastal areas managed for waterfowl.

Rabbits, raccoons, and opossums are found generally statewide.

Sinepuxent Bay, Ernest A. Vaughn, Ellis Bay, Deal Island, Fairmount, Cedar Island, Pocomoke Sound, Fishing Bay, and Taylor's Island are the primary waterfowl-management areas.

There is a place for the hunter in the Old Line State.

21 • MASSACHUSETTS—Birds, Deer, and Small Game

Small, with only 8,257 square miles, but heavily populated with almost six million people, Massachusetts is a surprisingly good hunting state—and a state where hunting is traditional.

A reasonably abundant white-tailed deer population and a smattering of black bears offer big-game hunting. There are brief seasons on both species.

A good variety of game birds may well be the state's best bet for the hunter, however. The ruffed-grouse hunting is excellent, but the ring-necked pheasant may be the state's most popular game bird. There is limited but good, quail hunting, and the woodcock hunting is good at times. Rails and snipes, rarely hunted, round out the game bird list.

The duck hunting is good, particularly for sea ducks, and there is limited goose hunting.

Gray squirrels are reasonably abundant, and cottontail rabbits are plentiful throughout the state. The snowshoe rabbit, however, is more sought after and probably receives more attention from the Division of Fisheries and Wildlife. There are foxes for the hound men and an abundance of raccoons for the night hunters. Woodchucks offer sport for the varmint hunters.

Federal lands are almost nonexistent in Massachusetts where most land is privately owned. Still, there is some public hunting on the Parker River National Wildlife Refuge, U.S. Corps of Engineers lands, National Park Service lands, and military lands, much under lease to the Massachusetts Division of Fisheries and Wildlife. Generally, though, the hunter must look to state or private lands for hunting opportunities.

The Massachusetts Division of Fisheries and Wildlife owns or leases approximately forty-five thousand acres of prime hunting land. There are, at this writing, approximately forty-five wildlife-management areas offering a wide variety of hunting. All are well-mapped, and copies of the maps can be obtained by writing the Information and Education Section, Massachusetts Division of Fisheries and Wildlife, Field Headquarters, Westboro, Massachusetts 01581. Enclose a stamped, self-addressed envelope. These areas range in size from two-hundred-acre Four Chimneys Wildlife Management Area to 6,000-acre Birch Hill Wildlife Management Area. Many of the areas are in excess of one thousand acres, however.

In addition to the wildlife-management areas there are an estimated 160,000 acres of state forests, many of which offer good hunting. The Division of Fisheries and Wildlife can supply information on these also.

With limited public hunting land, many hunters, residents particularly, look to the private lands for most of their hunting. The permission of the owner or tenant is needed to hunt lands posted with signs prohibiting hunting. The signs must bear the name of the owner or tenant. The law does not not indicate that written permission is needed, but that is the safest course.

The Berkshire Mountains offer the best deer hunting in the state as well as limited black-bear hunting. Good wildlife-management areas for the deer hunter include Birch Hill, Four Chimneys, Swift River, Winimusset Meadows, Quaboag River, Phillipston, Hubbardston, Middleboro, and Myles Standish.

The bird hunter will find good pheasant hunting on Swift River, West Hill, Winimusset Meadows, Quaboag River, Moose Hill, Hubbardston, Hodges Village, Rocky Gutter, Housatonic Valley, Knightville, Poland Brook, Stafford Hill, Harold Parker, Northeast, Crane, and Myles Standish Wildlife Management Areas.

Good grouse areas include Phillipston, Birch Hill, Peru, Canada Hill, Northeast, Harold Parker, Crane Pond, Rocky Gutter, Otis A.F.B., Hubbardston, Swift River, and Myles Standish.

The quail hunter will find fair hunting in the southeast, including the Myles Standish, Marconi Beach, Otis Air Force Base, Rocky Gutter, and Crane Wildlife Management Areas.

In addition to the woodcocks that nest in the state, Massachusetts is on a major woodcock migration route, and many of the wildlife-management areas offer good hunting. Among them are Swift River, Winimusset Meadows, West Hill, Quaboag River, Moose Hill, Hubbardston, Rocky Gutter, Poland Brook, Harold Parker, Canada Hill, Pantry Brook, Peru, Birch Hill, and Knightville.

Massachusetts hunters enjoy good woodcock hunting. *Courtesy of Bill Byrne.*

Most of the waterfowl areas offer good shooting for snipes and rails. Try Quaboag River, Rocky Gutter, Pantry Brook, Millers River, or Mill Creek Wildlife Management Areas.

All of the wildlife-management areas mentioned for snipes and rails are good for waterfowl, but others include West Hill, Hubbardston, Housatonic Valley, Northeast, Birch Hill, and West Meadows. Jump shooting along the inland rivers and hunting sea ducks off the coast are additional waterfowl possibilities. There is some public hunting on the Parker River National Wildlife Refuge.

Squirrels will be found just about all over the state and on many of the inland wildlife-management areas. Possibilities include West Meadows, Birch Hill, Northeast, Hubbardston, West Hill, Hodges Village, Crane Pond, Phillipston, Knightville, Four Chimneys, Peru, Becket, Harold Parker, Poland Brook, Swift River, Quaboag River, Rocky Gutter, and Millers River.

Cottontail rabbits also occur in abundance all over the state, but among the better wildlife-management areas are Millers River, Pantry Brook, Rocky Gutter, Quaboag River, Swift River, Winimusset Meadows, Moose Hill, Poland Brook, Stafford Hill, Canada Hill, Peru, Savoy, Four Chimneys, Westboro, Knightville, Crane, Hodges Village, Myles Standish, West Hill, Hubbardston, Housatonic, Northeast, West Hill, and Birch Hill.

The popular snowshoe hare is stocked on some of the wildlife-management areas, including Northeast, Hubbardston, Hodges Village, Phillipston, Four Chimneys, Savoy, Peru, Becket, Canada Hill, Harold Parker, and Moose Hill. These are probably the best areas for the big varying hares.

Night hunters will find good coon populations on many of the wildlife-management areas, including Quaboag River, Rocky Gutter, Millers River, Swift River, Winimusset Meadows, Moose Hill, Harold Parker, Peru, Savoy, Four Chimneys, Phillipston, Marconi Beach, Crane Pond, Myles Standish, Hubbardston, Northeast and Birch Hill.

Foxes occur just about all over the state, and woodchucks are found near the edges, on abandoned farms, and in the agricultural areas.

There is still good hunting in tradition-rich Massachusetts.

22 • MICHIGAN—For Bears and Deer

Divided by Lake Michigan, Lake Huron, and the famous Straits of Mackinac, Michigan's lake-dotted, fifty-eight thousand square miles support a bustling population of 8.9 million people. Most of its population is concentrated in the Lower Peninsula. Hunting is traditional in Michigan and its citizens enjoy a wide variety of very good hunting.

A flourishing deer herd and a modest black-bear population support big-game hunting in Michigan. Progress is being made on the restoration of the wild turkey, and at present, there is limited turkey hunting during a spring gobbler season. A few elk and moose are present, but not in huntable populations. Both are protected and have been for years.

Cottontail rabbits, snowshoe hares, and both fox and gray squirrels are the major small-game animals, but there is also hunting for bobcats, coyotes, foxes, raccoons, and woodchucks. Michigan is one of the few states that has open and closed seasons on woodchucks. There are also a few opossums and badgers.

The ruffed grouse is the most popular upland game bird in Michigan, and there is fair hunting in all parts of the state. Spruce grouse are protected, but there is fair sharptail hunting. There are a few prairie chickens, but they, too, are fully protected. The pheasant hunting is fair, and the woodcock hunting is excellent. A few bobwhite quail, snipes, and rails round out the game-bird hunting.

In spite of its vast open waters, duck hunting in Michigan is not truly great. Limited marshes, open shorelines, and forests limit the waterfowl habitat. This is not to say there is not good waterfowl hunting in the state. There is much fine hunting for both ducks and geese.

Federal lands are abundant in Michigan. Four national forests, two in the Upper Peninsula and two in the Lower Peninsula, provide a total of 2.6 million acres of public hunting land. On the Upper Peninsula in the west is 886,000-acre Ottawa National Forest. Write the Supervisor, Ottawa National Forest, Ironwood, Michigan 49938, for maps and hunting information. Further east on the Upper Peninsula is Hiawatha National Forest with 839,000 acres of public hunting land. The supervisor is located in Escanaba, Michigan 49829. This forest is divided into two sections. In the Lower Peninsula, there are 415,000-acre Huron National Forest and the Manistee National Forest with another 465,000 acres of prime hunting land. The supervisor for both National Forests is located in Cadillac, Michigan 49601.

State-owned lands are also vast in Michigan. Thirty state forests scattered over the Lower and Upper Peninsulas total 3.8 million acres of public hunting land, and several thousand acres are managed as wildlife-management areas. There are fifty-two state game areas, a half dozen state wildlife areas, and several state wildlife-research areas. Information on these areas, including maps showing graphically the location of all public hunting lands in Michigan, can be obtained from the Department of Natural Resources, Stevens Mason Building, Lansing, Michigan 48926.

In addition to the public lands owned by federal and state agencies, there are many acres of forest land open to public hunting because of the Forest Reserve Act, which relieves the owner of property taxes on such land so long as the timber is not harvested. Information on these lands can be obtained from the Department of Natural Resources.

There is also a good deal of excellent hunting on the many farms in the Lower Peninsula, but the hunter should consult the owners of farms or other private lands before entering them.

Michigan has long been one of the leading deer hunting states in the nation. Good whitetail hunting is found all over the state in both the Upper and Lower Peninsulas, but probably the very best deer hunting in the state, and some of the best in America, can be found in the north-central counties of the Lower Peninsula. The western and southwestern regions of the Upper Peninsula are also good. The farmlands of the southern part of the Lower Peninsula are noted for trophy bucks.

The black-bear kill, seldom large in Michigan, is usually heaviest on the Upper Peninsula, with the extreme western region being the best.

The wild turkey is struggling in Michigan, but the best hunting will now be found in the northern regions of the Lower Peninsula, where vast forests and a suitable climate favor the big bird. The Baldwin and Mio areas are likely the best bet for bagging a tom turkey.

The ruffed grouse is the most popular game bird in Michigan. *Courtesy of Michigan Department of Natural Resources.*

The ruffed grouse can be found in good cover all over the state, but the four national forests offer the best prospects for this top Michigan game bird. By far the best hunting is found in the forests of the Upper Peninsula and in the northern regions of the Lower Peninsula.

The pheasant hunting, once supreme in the state, is now fair at best. By far the best hunting will be found in the extreme southwestern part of the state, much of it on private land. There are some good public hunting areas in the Kalamazoo area, however, and among them are the Dansville, Gourdneck, and Lapeer State Game Areas.

Woodcock hunting is so good in Michigan that it is difficult to name a best area. Many birds nest in the northern region of the Lower Peninsula, but more important, this part of the state is on a major migration route of birds funneling south from Ontario and the Upper Peninsula. Grouse and woodcocks make a fine combination for a mixed bag hunt. The seasons usually run concurrently.

The only reasonably good sharptail hunting is found in the eastern part of the Upper Peninsula and on islands such as Drummond and Sugar in Lake Huron.

Quail hunting is generally limited to private lands, and snipes and rails are taken along the coasts.

Cottontails in the south and snowshoes in the north describe the rabbit picture, and gray squirrels in the dense forests and fox squirrels in the farm woodlots tell the bushy-tail story in Michigan.

The waterfowl hunting is good all over the state, with the Upper Peninsula leading the goose harvest, but the Lower Peninsula furnishing a larger percentage of the duck take.

Michigan continues to rank among the best as a hunting state.

23 • MINNESOTA—For Deer, Ducks, and Grouse

Minnesota is a big state. The hunter will drive a good four hundred miles from its southern border to reach the Canadian border. And east to west across the widest point is another four-hundred-mile trip. Minnesota is also a transition state. To the north, there are dense coniferous forests and sparkling lakes—true north country—but the hunter traveling from the Twin Cities area west to North Dakota traverse treeless plains country much like the North Dakota land he is headed for.

The state's three and one-half million people are spread pretty thin in places over its eighty-four thousand square miles.

Finding a place to hunt in Minnesota is rarely a problem, with approximately one-fourth of the land under specific ownership.

The white-tailed deer is Minnesota's top big-game animal, and a herd estimated at 450,000 animals is spread just about all over the state. The black bear, unprotected and considered a nuisance in the past, is now a big-game animal and gets more attention. Limited moose seasons held in 1971, 1973, and 1975 were the first in years. Elk are present in very limited numbers, but are not hunted.

Minnesota is also a top ruffed-grouse state, and there is good sharp-tailed grouse hunting in the northwest regions. The Hungarian partridge is well established, and the ring-necked pheasants furnish reasonably good hunting. There are good woodcock, snipe, and rail populations, but they receive very little attention. Prairie chickens, chukar, quail, and mourning doves are protected. Wild turkey hunters have just completed their first spring season ever.

Cottontails, jackrabbits, and snowshoe hares are plentiful in Minnesota, but they receive very little attention from hunters. Both gray and fox squirrels are reasonably abundant and could stand heavier hunting. Other animals include the red and gray foxes, raccoons, bobcats, lynx, badgers, and timber wolves.

Because it is a prime nesting area and also gets strong migration flights, Minnesota is an excellent waterfowl state. Both ducks and geese are plentiful, and the hunting interest is high.

Public hunting lands are almost equally divided between federal and state ownership.

Two large national forests comprise most of the Federal holdings in the state. The Chippewa in north-central Minnesota contains 640,000 acres of prime hunting land, with headquarters at Cass Lake, Minnesota 56633. Write there to the Supervisor, Chippewa National Forest, for hunting information and maps. The much larger Superior National Forest, with over two million acres of public land, part of which includes the Boundary Waters Canoe Area, is in the lake-rich northeastern part of the state. Write the Supervisor, Superior National Forest, Duluth, Minnesota 55801, for maps and hunting information.

There is also limited hunting on the Agassiz, Sherburne, Tamarac, and Upper Mississippi River National Wildlife Refuges.

With three million acres of land in fifty-four state forests, Minnesota offers almost unlimited hunting opportunities. Additionally, there are over one thousand tracts of land available in state and federal wildlife-management areas made up mostly of 848 wildlife-management-area wetlands. Full information on hunting these vast lands can be obtained by writing the Minnesota Department of Natural Resources, 390 Centennial Office Building, St. Paul, Minnesota 55155. Ask for a copy of a map called *Minnesota Wildlife Lands*.

With three and one-half million acres of public land, the Minnesota counties, collectively, are larger landowners than the federal government. Most of these county lands are open to public hunting.

In addition to the various federal, state, and county lands, several of the large pulp companies permit hunting on their lands, which total several thousand acres. The Department of Natural Resources can provide information on these lands or can provide the names and addresses of the corporate offices.

Under the Minnesota law, agricultural land containing standing crops is specifically protected against trespass, and the owner is not required to post such land. Wooded areas, other than tree farms, are not considered agricultural lands, but the hunter should play it safe and ask permission—particularly if the area is in farming country or near human habitation.

Minnesota is an excellent waterfowl state. *Photo by Bob Gooch.*

The best deer hunting is found in north-central and northwestern Minnesota, but there is reasonably good hunting all over the state.

Northeastern Minnesota offers the best bear hunting, and the northern counties of Beltrami, Cook, Kittson, and Marshall are the best bets for the limited moose hunting that is available in Minnesota.

While ruffed grouse are widely distributed in Minnesota, the very best hunting is in the southern part of the northern forest regions. Both of the national forests offer top grouse hunting, and most of the state forests are located in prime ruffed-grouse range.

Sharp-tailed grouse are found primarily in the extreme northwest, and the introduced Hungarian partridge has fared best in the southwestern agricultural areas. The counties along the South Dakota border offer probably the best Hun territory in the state.

Ring-necked pheasants occupy much the same range as the Hun, but the best hunting is in the southeastern region from Minneapolis-St. Paul south to the Iowa border. Generally though, the ringneck may be found in varying degrees of abundance throughout the southern half of the state.

Among them the cottontail, jackrabbit, and snowshoe provide good hunting throughout Minnesota. The best cottontail-range is in the southwestern quarter of the state. The jackrabbit occupies pretty much the same territory, but it is not found in the southeast where the cottontail is reasonably abundant. The snowshoe is most abundant among the vast coniferous forests of the north—particularly the northeast.

Both gray and fox squirrels are found in the southern half of the state, though they prefer different habitats. The gray likes the dense hardwood forests while the fox prefers the farming country woodlots.

The waterfowl hunting is so uniformly good in Minnesota that it is difficult to pinpoint the best areas. Ducks and geese are found everywhere, and the 860 wildlife-management areas offer plenty of hunting opportunities. The national wildlife refuges—Agassiz, Sherburne, Tamarac, and Upper Mississippi River—are worth investigating.

The hunter who lives in Minnesota is fortunate indeed.

24 • MISSISSIPPI—For Southern Hunting

Doves and quail for the bird hunter, rabbits and squirrels for the small-game enthusiast, and deer and turkeys for the big-game hunter are the offerings of Mississippi, deep in the South and bordering the Gulf of Mexico. With a population of two and one-half million people and a land area of 47,716 square miles, Mississippi is a popular hunting state for residents and nonresidents alike.

The bobwhite quail and mourning dove vie for the number one spot among Mississippi hunters. Both species provide good hunting, but the bobwhite populations are dropping slightly, while doves are on the increase. The squirrel probably outranks the rabbit as the number one game animal in Mississippi, but both are extremely popular and found just about statewide. The deer herds are on the increase, and the wild turkey, once unbelievably abundant, is making a strong comeback. The waterfowl hunting is generally good. Other game includes woodcocks, snipes, and rails, with raccoons and opossums for the night hunters.

With six national forests within its borders, Mississippi has millions of acres of federal land available for public hunting. The national forests are well spaced throughout the state. Starting in the north there is Holly Springs, and then Tombigbee, Delta, and Bienville near the center of the state, with Homochitto and DeSoto in the south. Collectively, they offer well over two million acres of public hunting land. DeSoto, with over one-half million acres, is the largest. Maps and hunting information on all Mississippi national forests can be obtained by writing the U.S. National Forests Supervisor, Jackson, Mississipi 39205. Other major federal lands include those adjacent to the U.S. Army Corps of Engineers reservoirs. All offer waterfowl hunting. Further information can be obtained by writing the Area Manager, 105 Madison Street, Calhoun City, MS 38916, for Arkabutla and Grenada Reservoirs; the Area Manager at Route 2, Collinsville, MS 39325, for Okatibbee Reservoir; and the Area Manager, Route 3, Box 85, Oxford, MS 38655, for Sardis Reservoir. There are also two National Wildlife Refuges in the state—Noxubee at Route 1, Brooksville, MS 39739, and Yazoo at Box 286, Hollandale, MS 38748. Both are under the jurisdiction of the U. S. Fish and Wildlife Service. Many of these lands are managed by the Mississippi Game and Fish Commission in cooperation with the federal agencies. Additional information can be obtained by writing the commission at P.O. Box 451, Jackson, Mississippi 39205.

Even without these vast federal lands, the hunter would find plenty of prime public hunting on the Mississippi wildlife-management areas. There are a total of twenty-one such areas providing over one and one-half million acres of well-managed game lands. Additionally, there are nine waterfowl areas on which public hunting is permitted. An attractive little folder called *Hunt in Mississippi* can be obtained from the commission at the above address. It describes and locates these areas. The commission also has more detailed information on individual wildlife-management areas. Finally, there is the Pearl River Waterfowl and Upland Game Area managed by the Pearl River Valley Water Supply District from headquarters at P. O. Box 131, Canton, Mississippi 39046.

As is the case in many southern states, private lands support the bulk of the hunting, and much of it on lands leased to hunting clubs. But there is a great deal of commercial forest land in the state on which hunters are welcome. Some offers possibly the very best hunting in Mississippi. The International Paper Company alone has almost 900,000 acres of land. Information on hunting these lands is available from the International Paper Company, Southern Kraft Division, P. O. Box Drawer A, Mobile, Alabama 36601. The St. Regis Paper Company, 150 East Forty Second Street, New York, New York 10017, also has land in Mississippi that is available for public hunting. These are the major companies, but information on others can be obtained from the Mississippi Game and Fish Commission. While the hunter needs permission to enter private lands, this is rarely a problem if the landowner is approached courteously. Most of the dove hunting is on private lands, as is the better quail and small-game hunting.

Even though the better quail hunting in Mississippi is on farmland, the timber-management practices of the pulp companies provide thousands of acres of prime hunting. There is also reasonably good quail hunting on several of the wildlife-management areas. Included are

Mourning doves are on the increase in Mississippi. *Photo by Bob Gooch.*

Bucatunna Creek, Shubuta-Stonewall, Calhoun County, Chickasaw, Choctaw, Copiah County, Issaquena County, John Bell Williams, Marion County, Red Creek, Upper Sardis, and Wolf River. The quail hunter might ask for specific information on several when writing the commission.

Doves will also be found on Bucatunna, Shubuta-Stonewall, Copiah County, Issaquena County, Marion County, Red Creek, and Wolf River. There is also good dove hunting on the Yazoo National Wildlife Refuge.

Both fox and gray squirrels are found in Mississippi, and just about all of the wildlife-management areas offer squirrel hunting, as do the national wildlife refuges. Squirrels are found throughout the state, however, wherever there is suitable habitat. Rabbits, both cottontail and swamp rabbits, are found on public as well as private lands, with the best cottontail hunting in farming country. The swamp rabbit is most common along the Mississippi River.

The best turkey hunting is in the southern half of Mississippi, where the national forests provide fair hunting. The better wildlife-management areas include Sandy Creek, Bienville, Bucatunna, Shubuta-Stonewall, Chickasawhay, Choctaw, Copiah County, Homochitto, Issaquena County, Leaf River, Little Biloxi, Malmaison, Red Creek, Sunflower, Tallahala Creek, and Wolf River. The Noxubee National Wildlife Refuge also offers fair turkey hunting.

The best deer hunting in the past has been along the Mississippi River, but much of the better hunting territory is controlled by private hunt clubs. Finding a place to hunt deer is no real problem, however, as all of the six national forests are good. So are the two national wildlife refuges and the great majority of the wildlife-management areas. In fact, there are deer on every one of the wildlife-management areas.

In addition to the waterfowl areas on the Corps of Engineers Reservoirs, the commission owns and manages Indian Bayou, Leflore County O'Keefe, and Yellow Creek Waterfowl Areas.

Few Mississippians complain about their hunting.

25 • MISSOURI—For Small Game

Missouri, 69,686 square miles of rolling hills, flat delta country, prairies, and stunted mountains, is country for the rabbit hunter and his beagles, the squirrel man, and the quail hunter and his brace of stylish pointers or setters. These popular species top an impressive list of game birds and animals that have long kept Missouri among the leading hunting states.

Hunters bag an estimated three million quail annually in Missouri, and on the basis of the harvest, the bobwhite tops all other game animals and birds in the state.

Mourning doves are also abundant, and there is some pheasant hunting in the northwestern part of the state. Both the ruffed grouse and prairie chicken, once abundant, are fully protected. Woodcocks, snipes, and rails are present in scattered areas of the state.

The waterfowl hunting is good in the lowlands, with mallards and Canada geese making up the bulk of the kill.

Both deer and wild turkeys, once abundant, are making comebacks under the watchful eye of the Missouri Department of Conservation. The black bear, though not truly rare, is fully protected.

Raccoons and opossums are popular among night hunters and are plentiful in suitable habitats throughout the state.

Woodchucks, coyotes, red and gray foxes, and bobcats round out the long list of game animals and birds in Missouri.

Two national forests, 768,254-acre Clark National Forest and 608,719-acre Mark Twain National Forest, were combined into the Mark Twain National Forest in 1976. This big national forest in the southern part of the state offers the biggest chunk of public hunting land

111

in Missouri. Maps and hunting information are available from the Forest Supervisor, Rolla, Missouri 65401.

The Swan Lake National Wildlife Refuge in the north-central part of the state offers hunting for geese. Information on hunting possibilities there can be obtained from the Missouri Department of Conservation, North Ten Mile Drive, Jefferson City, Missouri 65101.

There are an estimated 200,000 acres of state forests in Missouri. All of them—Alley Spring, Beal, Blair Creek, Carrs Creek, Cardareva, Clearwater, Cedar Grove, Clow Tract, Dickens Valley, Elmslie, Elm Spring, Coldwater, Daniel Boone, Deer Run, Huckleberry Ridge, Logan Creek, Indian Trail, Huzzah, Paint Rock, Powder Mill, Rocky Creek, Fourche Creek, Little Black, Reifsnider, Sugar Creek, Poplar Bluff, Shannondale, Riverside, and others—are open to public hunting. For complete information, write the Department of Conservation.

While the state forests comprise a big block of public hunting land, there are also many acres in wildlife areas and sites and tracts. Write the Department of Conservation for information. These areas are scattered widely through the state.

The Department of Conservation is constantly adding to its state forests and wildlife areas as suitable land at a reasonable price becomes available.

The Department of Conservation also manages twelve thousand acres of Federal lands in the Upper Mississippi Wildlife Management Area with ten thousand open to public hunting.

While there is a good deal of public hunting land in Missouri, over 90 percent of the state is in private ownership. Possibly the very best hunting in the state is found on private lands. I went to Missouri several autumns ago for the specific purpose of hunting the big fox squirrels, and I went armed with complete information on all available public hunting land—particularly that noted for its squirrel hunting. But, except for one morning in the Mark Twain National Forest, I spent the entire hunting trip on the private lands of the owner of the campground my wife and I set up camp in.

As in most states, trespass for the purpose of hunting is illegal in Missouri, and some landowners strictly enforce the law. Generally, finding good hunting territory on private lands is not difficult. Small-game hunting for rabbits and squirrels and bird hunting for doves and quail are often best on farmland. The hunter striking out on his own without asking permission is courting trouble, however. A polite inquiry may open many acres of fine hunting.

The bulk of the quail kill comes from the Northeast River Breaks,

The cottontail rabbit is one of the top game animals in Missouri. *Courtesy of Don Wooldridge.*

Ozark Plateau, west Ozark border, and western prairie regions of the state—and from farmlands not worked too intensively. There is good quail hunting on the wildlife areas, however. Included among the better ones are the Atlanta, Bonanza, Brickyard Hill, and Danville Wildlife Areas. Also good are Gainesville, Honey Creek, Neeper, and Schell-Osaga.

The best rabbit hunting is found north of the Missouri River and on the Western Prairie Region. Rabbits are actually found in every one of the 114 counties in the state.

Like rabbits, squirrels are abundant in Missouri and are found all over the state. The Missouri hunter seldom has to go far for prime squirrel hunting, and both the fox, called "Big Red" in the state, and the little gray are abundant.

The best gray squirrel hunting occurs in the dense forests of the Ozarks and along the Mississippi River and other bottomlands. The fox is most abundant north of the Missouri River and in the western part of the state, where open woodlands favor its kind of living. Both national forests and most of the wildlife areas, as well as the state forests, offer good squirrel hunting.

Doves are also found statewide, but the best hunting is in the southeast Boothill region and in the western farming country. There is also good hunting in the various rich valley farmlands. Good wildlife areas include Atlanta, Bonanza, Gainesville, Pigeon Hill, Prairie Home, and Schell-Osage.

In addition to the Swan Lake National Wildlife Refuge, good waterfowl hunting is found along both the Missouri and Mississippi Rivers. The better waterfowling wildlife areas include Schell-Osage, Duck Creek, Fountain Grove, Montrose, and Trimble. There is also good waterfowl hunting on Lake Wappapello, a state recreation area. Jump shooting is good on many Missouri streams.

The national forests offer good deer hunting, although much of the best whitetail hunting is found on private lands. Benton, Gasconade, Ozark, and Texas counties often lead the state in the deer kill. Good wildlife areas include August Busch, Rudolf Bennett, Ted Shanks, Deer Ridge, and Trimble.

Turkey hunting is now open in seventy-nine Missouri counties, with the national forest lands and state forests in those open counties the best bet for bagging a gobbler. The national forests and the Bozarth and Daniel Boone Memorial State Forests offer good public hunting.

There is plenty of good hunting in the "Show-Me" state.

26 • MONTANA—For Big Game and Sage Grouse

Straddling the Continental Divide, mountainous and rugged in the West and with a vast plains area in the East, Montana is truly a hunter's paradise. At 147,000 square miles, Montana is big, and its 700,000 people have plenty of elbow room and wide open spaces.

The big western state is a big-game hunter's state, and the only one of the lower forty-eight states still offering hunting for grizzly bears. Other popular big-game species include both white-tailed and mule deer, antelope, elk, black bears, moose, sheep, goats, and mountain lions.

Though big game dominates the hunting picture, there is surprisingly good sharp-tailed grouse and sage grouse hunting on the eastern plains—bird hunting much like that found in North Dakota to the east. Other game birds include ring-necked pheasant, Hungarian and chukar partridge, ruffed, blue, and spruce grouse, and wild turkeys.

For the waterfowler, there are snipes, swans, ducks, and geese. The Pacific and Central Flyways share Montana.

There are cottontails, jackrabbits, and snowshoe hares for the small-game hunter, plus coyotes, wolverines, bobcats, lynx, weasels, badgers, raccoons, red foxes, porcupines, and a variety of other animals.

Federal lands abound in Montana, and they serve as a reservoir for most hunting. They include national forests and Bureau of Land Management lands, Indian Reservations, Bureau of Reclamation lands, and lands of the Fish and Wildlife Service.

The most important—for the big-game hunter, particularly—are the eleven national forests totaling over sixteen million acres. Collectively, they also provide five primitive areas and four wilderness areas. Beaverhead National Forest is headquartered at Dillon, MT 59725;

Bitterroot at Hamilton, MT 59840; Custer at Billings, MT 59103; Deer Lodge at Butte, MT 59701; Flathead at Kalispell, MT 59901; Gallatin at Bozeman, MT 59715; Helena at Helena, MT 59601; Kaniksu at Sandpoint, ID 83864; Kootenai at Libby, MT 59923; Lewis and Clark at Great Falls, MT 59401; and Lolo at Missoula, MT 59801. Beaverhead and Flathead are vast national forests, both boasting over two million acres of public hunting lands. Bitterroot, Deer Lodge, Kottenai, Lewis and Clark, and Gallatin contain over one million acres each, and Helena, just under one million acres.

Montana shares Custer with South Dakota, and Kaniksu and Lolo with Idaho, but these three forests provide millions of acres of additional public hunting land in the state. A letter to the forest supervisor at the addresses given above will bring complete hunting information and excellent maps.

The Bureau of Land Management also owns several hundred thousand acres of land in Montana. Much of it is in the eastern part of the state, offering excellent hunting for antelope, sharp-tailed grouse, sage grouse, and Hungarian partridge. Information and maps can be obtained by writing to the Bureau of Land Management, 3021 Sixth Avenue North, Box 30157, Billings, Montana 59103. An excellent map showing in color all public lands in Montana is available from this office.

Information on the lands of the U. S. Fish and Wildlife Service can be obtained from the Bureau of Sport Fisheries and Wildlife, Missouri River Basin Studies, 711 Central Avenue, Billings, Montana 59101, and on the lands of the Bureau of Reclamation from 316 North Twenty-Sixth Street, Billings, Montana 59101.

The Blackfeet, Flathead, Rocky Boy, Fort Belknap, Fort Peck, Northern Cheyenne, and Crow Indian reservations also offer public hunting opportunities. Details can be obtained from the Bureau of Indian Affairs, 316 North Twenty-Sixth Street, Billings, Montana 59101.

State-owned lands are not nearly so extensive as the federal ones, but with so much land under public ownership, there has not been a great need for state-owned lands. Still, the Coal Creek, Lincoln, Stillwater, Sula, Swan River, Thompson River, and Clearwater State Forests do provide additional public hunting opportunities. Information on these lands and on game-management areas and game ranges administered by the Montana Department of Fish and Game can be obtained by writing that office at Helena, Montana 59601.

Montana is a truly great deer-hunting state, with both white-tailed and mule deer abundant, though the muley fortunes have faded a bit in recent years. While the whitetail hunting is good just about statewide,

The antelope is just one of the big-game animals Montana is noted for. *Photo by Bob Gooch.*

the best mule-deer hunting is found east of the Continental Divide. Public hunting land is abundant for both white-tailed and mule deer, and locating good hunting is no problem.

In general, the southeast offers the best antelope hunting, and there is a great deal of Bureau of Land Management land in that area.

Montana is one of the best elk states, and the national forests offer almost unlimited hunting opportunities. All are good.

Moose are generally limited to the southwestern region, and both sheep and goats are found in the mountains north of Yellowstone National Park. Most grizzly bears are found in the north in the vicinity of Glacier National Park. Black bears are fairly abundant and are found throughout the forested regions.

The wild turkey hunting is limited, but the best of what is available is in the southeast, where the Custer National Forest offers good hunting opportunities.

Southeastern Montana also offers the best ring-necked pheasant hunting, though pheasant hunting is not truly good anywhere in the state—except for unusual years.

The sharp-tailed grouse is the top game bird in Montana, followed closely by the bigger sage grouse. It is quite abundant in the central and eastern regions where Bureau of Land Management land offers good public hunting. The sage grouse is also found in pretty much the same general area as the sharptail, though it is attracted to sagebrush flats instead of the brushy prairies the sharptail loves. The Hungarian partridge is probably the most widely distributed bird in the state, and the hunting is excellent in the north-central region. Blue and ruffed grouse are reasonably abundant in the high country forests, and locating good territory in the national and state forests is no great problem.

The eastern wheatlands draw many geese. Mallards are the most popular duck, and they occur all over the state.

Hunting is great in the Big Sky state.

27 • NEBRASKA—Deer, Pheasants, and Waterfowl

A land of sweeping plains, broken hill country, and picturesque sand hills, Nebraska is 77,227 square miles of fine hunting country. It is home to over one and one-half million Americans.

The Nebraska big-game hunter will find excellent hunting for both mule and white-tailed deer, good wild turkey hunting, and limited hunting for antelope.

For the bird hunter, there is excellent dove hunting, good pheasant hunting, populations of both sharp-tailed grouse and prairie chickens, and fair-to-good quail hunting. There are also snipes and rails.

An abundance of cottontail rabbits provides fine sport for the small-game hunter, and there is fair squirrel hunting. Fox squirrels make up the bulk of the state's squirrel populations. Coyotes, bobcats, raccoons, foxes, jackrabbits, and prairie dogs round out the small-game possibilities.

Some of the very best waterfowl hunting in the Central Flyway can be found in Nebraska, with duck hunters bagging over a quarter of a million birds, and the goose harvest in the neighborhood of fifteen to twenty thousand. Canadas, blues, and snows are the major geese. Mallards comprise the bulk of the duck harvest, followed by teal, pintails, and scaup.

While most of Nebraska is under private ownership, there are many square miles of excellent public hunting. The 250,000-acre Nebraska National Forest provides much prime hunting land, particularly in the Pine Ridge Area. Maps and hunting information can be obtained from the Forest Supervisor, Nebraska National Forest, 270 Pine Street, Chadron, Nebraska 69337.

The Oglala National Grasslands in the northwestern part of the state offers prairie hunting. Information and maps are available from the forest supervisor at Chadron.

Important to waterfowl hunters in particular, but also to other hunters as well, are the federal waterfowl-production areas, forty in number and ranging in size from 43 acres up to 1,485. Good maps and hunting information are available from the Bureau of Sports Fisheries and Wildlife, Federal Building, Fort Snelling, Twin Cities, Minnesota 55111, or from the Nebraska Game and Parks Commission P.O. Box 30370, Lincoln, Nebraska 68503. There is also limited hunting on a few military lands and Indian Reservations, but their status changes frequently, so it is best to check before hunting them. The Game and Parks Commission is a good place to start. The commission can also provide information on U.S. Army Corps of Engineers lands and national wildlife refuges. Both the Crescent Lake and Valentine National Wildlife Refuges are sizeable.

State-owned hunting lands are numerous and support much of the public hunting. These areas are classified as either *special-use areas* or *state recreation areas*. They are found all over the state, but are particularly numerous in the southwestern section.

The recreation areas are often closed to hunting at certain times of the year, but are generally open for dove hunting on September 1 and for other species beginning October 1. These state-owned areas range in size from five-acre Plum Creek Special-Use Area to 21,000-acre Fort Robinson State Park. Complete information on these hunting lands is available from the commission.

As in most states, private lands also support a good deal of Nebraska hunting, but the permission of the landowner is required before hunting any private lands.

The mule deer is an inhabitant of western Nebraska. The famous Pine Ridge Area of the Nebraska National Forest is a popular area for muley hunters. It offers forty-nine thousand acres of forest and plains hunting. Other good areas include the James Ranch Special-Use Area in the Panhandle, Pine Glen Wildlife Special-Use Area in the Sand Hills, and Medicine Creek Special-use Area in the southwest.

The top white-tailed deer hunting is in the eastern part of the state, with the very best in the southeast. Likely areas include Pawnee Prairie Special-Use Area and Indian Cave State Park.

Though limited in area, the antelope hunting is good in Nebraska. The best is on private lands, but both the Crescent Lake National Wildlife Refuge and Oglala National Grasslands offer antelope hunting.

A trio of happy Nebraska squirrel hunters. *Courtesy of Nebraska Game Commission.*

The introduced Merriam's turkey is the principal wild turkey in Nebraska, with reasonably good hunting available in the Pine Ridge Area of the Nebraska National Forest. Other good public hunting areas include the Ponderosa, Gilbert-Baker, and Metcalf Special-Use Areas.

The ring-necked pheasant is Nebraska's most sought after game species. Birds are abundant in most years. By far the best hunting will be found in the farmland, and thus on private lands. Generally, the eastern counties produce the best hunting. Good public hunting areas are numerous—County Line Marsh, Krause Lagoon and Wilkins Lagoon Federal Waterfowl Production Areas, Bluestem Lake Recreation Area, and Cornhusker and Pawnee Prairie Special-Use Areas.

Quail are found along most stream courses, with the southeast providing the best hunting. Nebraska is on the northern fringe of the quail's range, however, and populations bounce up and down with the often-harsh Nebraska winters.

The Sand Hills Region is the best bet for both prairie chickens and sharp-tailed grouse, though these grasslands grouse may occur throughout the north-central region. Both private lands and state special-use areas in this region provide hunting for both chickens and sharptails. The huge Valentine National Wildlife Refuge is a good possibility.

The more common fox squirrel is found in suitable habitat all over the state. Just about any wooded public-hunting area should offer fair squirrel hunting. The smaller gray is most abundant along the Missouri River bottoms. Cottontail rabbits are also found just about statewide, with the best hunting in the privately owned farmlands.

The best public waterfowl hunting will be found on the federal waterfowl-production areas that are scattered rather widely over the state. Those in the Sand Hills Region, the prairie pothole-country, and the Rainwater Basin in the southeast are among the best.

A good hunter can spend a busy lifetime in Nebraska.

28 • NEVADA—For Desert Hunting

With 85 percent of its 110,540 square miles in the public domain, finding a place to hunt in Nevada is rarely a problem. Much of the state's big game is limited to residents only, however. Most of Nevada's population of slightly over one-half million people is scattered pretty thinly over this picturesque western land of deserts and mountains. Many of them live in several major cities.

The big-game offering is varied. Antelope and elk are limited to residents only, but the visiting hunter can draw for mule deer, cougars and bighorn sheep. Wild turkeys can be hunted by residents only.

There is an even wider variety of game for the bird hunter. The chukar partridge is the leading game bird, but the mountain quail is native to the state, and there are good populations of introduced valley, Gambel's, and scaled quail. Limited pheasant hunting, a few Hungarian partridge, good mourning-dove populations, a smattering of white-winged doves, snipes, good sage-grouse hunting, and limited blue grouse round out the game bird list.

Rabbits are the principal small game. There are both cottontail and pygmy rabbits, plus an abundance of jackrabbits, including both the black-tailed jack and the larger whitetail. Both bobcats and coyotes are fairly plentiful, particularly in good rabbit country. Bobcats are limited to resident trappers, however.

For an arid state, the waterfowl hunting is surprisingly good, with mallards abundant, coots, geese, mergansers, and limited hunting for whistling swans.

Nevada's two national forests, the Humboldt and Toiyabe National Forests, offer a combined total of over five million acres of public hunting land. Nevada shares Toiyabe with California. Maps and hunting information on Humboldt are available from the Forest Supervisor, Humboldt National Forest, Elko, Nevada 89801, and the Forest Supervisor, Toiyabe National Forest, Reno, Nevada 89501, can provide the same information on that national forest.

Other federal lands include vast tracts of Bureau of Land Management and Reclamation Bureau lands. The Nevada Department of Fish and Game, Box 10678, Reno, Nevada 89501, can supply information on these lands.

Additional federal lands on which some public hunting is permitted include the Fallon, Ruby Lake, and Winnemucca National Wildlife Refuges, Sheldon Antelope Range, Desert and Pahranagat National Wildlife Ranges, the Spring Mountain Range, and certain portions of the U. S. Air Force Bombing and Gunnery Range. The Department of Fish and Game can provide details on hunting these federal lands.

Lands owned and managed by the Nevada Department of Fish and Game include the Mason Valley, Scripps, Fernley, Overton, Wayne E. Kirch, Key-Pittman, Stillwater, Humboldt, and Overton-Key Wildlife Management Areas. Most of the state lands are managed primarily for waterfowl. Information on these areas can be obtained by writing to the Department of Fish and Game.

With only 15 percent of the state under private ownership, there is little need to hunt on private lands, but such permission is generally not hard to obtain. There is some public hunting on the lands of the Sierra Pacific Power Company, but much of it is posted. The Department of Fish and Game can supply information on these lands.

Mule deer are found in all of the state's seventeen counties, but Elko is the top deer-hunting county. Humboldt County is also good. Both are in the northern part of the state along the Idaho and Oregon borders. The Humboldt National Forest provides good public hunting land in both counties. The Jarbridge Wilderness Area of the Elko County portion of the Humboldt National Forest is a good possibility.

Western Humboldt County is the prime antelope range, and the Sheldon Antelope Range is located there.

The Humboldt National Forest in White Pine County is a good choice for the state's limited elk hunting. The bighorn-sheep hunting is also extremely limited and confined primarily to the Desert Game Range just north of Las Vegas. Mountain lions are found statewide. The only populations of wild turkeys are in Douglas and Washoe Counties.

The quail hunter will find good mountain-quail hunting in the counties of Humboldt, Washoe, Mineral, and Esmeralda; good valley-quail

Nevada has good populations of mourning doves and a few whitewings. *Photo by Bob Gooch.*

populations in the counties of Churchill, Humboldt, White Pine, and Washoe; Gambel's quail in the desert regions of Clark, Lincoln, and Nye; and scaled-quail hunting in Nye County. Elko and Humboldt Counties are good choices for both Hungarian partridge and chukar partridge. Clark and Nye Counties are the top dove regions, and the Fernley Wildlife Management Area in Nye is a good bet for public hunting. Elko and Humboldt Counties normally produce the best sage-grouse harvests. The Humboldt National Forest provides plenty of public hunting land in these counties, and the Humboldt National Forest areas of Elko, White Pine, and Lincoln Counties offer public hunting for the blue grouse.

Rabbits are found all over the state, and the small-game hunter will experience little trouble finding good territory for bunny-busting.

Good waterfowl counties include Churchill, Lyon, Pershing, Clark, and Washoe. There are also a number of good wildlife-management areas including Stillwater, Fernley, Overton, Humboldt, Mason Valley, Key Pittman, and the Ruby Lake National Wildlife Refuge. The

Pahranagat National Wildlife Refuge also provides some public hunting for waterfowl.

There is much interesting hunting in Nevada, but with antelope, elk, sage grouse, blue grouse, pheasants, bobcats, and turkeys limited to residents of the state, and a limited number of mule deer, cougars and bighorn sheep permits allotted to nonresidents, it is not a good state for the visiting hunter.

29 • NEW HAMPSHIRE—For Forest Hunting

New Hampshire, 9,304 square miles of rich forests, rugged mountains, fast rivers, and sparkling lakes, is a joy to hunt. While many of its almost 800,000 citizens are avid outdoorsmen and hunters, nonresidents make up 15 percent of the hunting population. With well over 85 percent of the state in woodlands, forest hunting ranks high.

The principal big-game animals are the white-tailed deer and the black bear. Deer are plentiful in just about all parts of the state, and there is much quality back-country hunting. Bears are most common in the three northern counties along the Ossipee Mountain Range. The moose herd is increasing, but at present there is no open season.

Bills now before the legislature could set seasons on both foxes and bobcats, now unprotected. Both are popular with hunters and, like the bear, are hunted with packs of crack trail hounds.

The ruffed grouse tops the game-bird list, and the extensive forest habitat is nearly ideal for this woodland grouse. The state has a good resident population of woodcocks and is on the major migration route of the birds. New Hampshire is near the border of the range of the ring-necked pheasant, but good hunting is maintained by stocking the gaudy birds. Ducks, geese, and snipes round out the bird hunting.

Hares, rabbits, and squirrels furnish good small-game hunting, and there is an abundance of raccoons for the night hunter.

Big 600,000-acre White Mountain National Forest blankets much of the north-central part of the state and offers some of the best woods hunting in New Hampshire. Maps and hunting information can be obtained by writing the forest headquarters at Laconia, New Hampshire 03246.

Other federal areas opened to public hunting in cooperation with the New Hampshire Fish and Game Department include Franklin Falls, Hopkinton-Everett, and Surry Mountain flood-control areas. Hunting information is available from the New Hampshire Fish and Game Department, 34 Bridge Street, New Hampshire 03301.

For years the Fish and Game Department has been acquiring wetlands and developing them as waterfowl-management areas. The department has also been acquiring upland management-areas for public hunting. There are now fifty such tracts scattered throughout the state. An excellent pamphlet called *Wildlife Management Area Guide* can be obtained by writing the Fish and Game Department at the above address. It describes each area in detail, lists the game to be expected, and tells the hunter how to reach the area.

Finally, some hunting is permitted in the state forests and parks. More complete information is available from the New Hampshire Division of Parks, Concord, New Hampshire 03301.

Private corporations own several million acres of New Hampshire land, most of it in commercial forests. Public hunting is generally permitted. The names and addresses of these corporations can be obtained from the Fish and Game Department. Major ones include the New England Power Company, 441 Stuart Street, Boston, Massachusetts 20016, and the St. Regis Paper Company, 150 East Forty-Second Street, New York, New York 10017.

Thanks to a cooperative deer-yard management program on both public and private lands and the efforts of game-damage technicians to prevent crop damage by game species, New Hampshire has an amazingly small amount of land posted against hunting. The posting law is simple. If private cultivated land is posted, permission is needed to hunt it.

Following record deer-kills of twelve thousand and fourteen thousand animals in 1967 and 1968, the New Hampshire deer harvest dropped dangerously, but it is on the upswing again following a number of consecutive mild winters. Carroll and Grafton Counties lead the state. Hunters average over one deer per square mile in these two counties. Both counties include big chunks of the White Mountain National Forest.

Carroll and Grafton also offer good bear hunting, as does Coos County. Bears are quite common north of Mount Cardigan in western New Hampshire and along the Ossipee Mountain Range in the East.

Both foxes and bobcats are found throughout the state, though the bobcat prefers the wilderness areas. Gray foxes are fairly abundant in the southern half of New Hampshire.

Stocking by the Fish and Game Department helps maintain fair pheasant hunting in New Hampshire. *Photo by Bob Gooch.*

Raccoon hunters also enjoy fair hunting throughout the state.

Cottontail rabbits, once plentiful in the southern half of the state, are now scarce, but the region is rich in gray squirrel populations. Snowshoe hares are abundant in the northern regions of New Hampshire and good hunting can be found in the White Mountain National Forest and other densely forested regions.

The ruffed grouse, or partridge as it is called in New England, is the number one game bird in New Hampshire and is found throughout the state. Abandoned farms reverting slowly to wild growth are particularly good. Probably the best grouse hunting will be found in the northern regions of the state in Coos County, part of which is in the White Mountain National Forest.

The Fish and Game Department stocks approximately seven thousand pheasants annually to boost the limited natural reproduction. Most are released in the farming country in the southern half of New Hampshire. The Merrimack River and the lower Connecticut River Valleys offer prime ring-necked pheasant habitat.

The woodcock, the second most popular game bird in the state, is also found statewide, but in most years it is particularly abundant in the seacoast areas and far to the north in Coos County.

Black ducks, wood ducks, goldeneyes, teal, and mergansers are the major resident ducks, and they support the bulk of the waterfowl hunting. Scoters are found along the coast. New Hampshire is in the Atlantic Flyway, and migrations of ducks boost the resident populations. Canada geese are making a comeback in the state, as they are everywhere. Jump shooting on the hundreds of wilderness ponds, beaver ponds, and rivers and marshes is extremely popular. The state has fourteen miles of oceanfront where blind hunting is popular. Great Bay and Little Bay are the top waterfowling spots. The Connecticut River is also good.

Big-game hunters, bird hunters, waterfowlers, night hunters, and small-game hunters will all find New Hampshire a joy to hunt.

30 • NEW JERSEY—Quail, Woodcocks, and Waterfowl

Almost within the long shadows of the New York City skyscrapers, populous New Jersey provides an amazing amount of good hunting. And some of the most enthusiastic hunters in America live in this small Atlantic Coast state. Only 7,839 square miles, it is home to over seven million Americans.

The white-tailed deer is the only big-game animal present in huntable numbers, but New Jersey hunters take twelve thousand deer annually, some within fifteen miles of New York City. The black bear populations probably do not exceed twenty-five animals, and bears have been protected since the 1950's.

The bobwhite-quail hunting is quite good, and the state has one of the best woodcock areas on the east coast. There are good pheasant populations, and ruffed-grouse hunting produces a respectable harvest annually. There are also a few chukars, mostly on private land. Snipe and reasonably good rail hunting round out the game bird possibilities.

The cottontail rabbit is the most popular game animal in New Jersey and it occurs in an abundance. There are also a few snowshoe hares and black-tailed jackrabbits. Gray squirrels are reasonably abundant. A good raccoon population, fair numbers of foxes, woodchucks, and opossums round out the small-game list.

With its long coastline, New Jersey has long been famous as a waterfowl state. Hunters take ducks, mergansers, sea ducks, brant, and geese.

Federal lands in New Jersey include some military lands on which limited hunting is permitted—27,000-acre Delaware Water Gap National Recreation Area, Brigantine National Wildlife Refuge, and Great Swamp National Wildlife Refuge. Most of the Delaware Water Gap National Recreation Area is open to public hunting for various species of game, and portions of the Brigantine National Wildlife Refuge are open to waterfowl hunting. Special deer hunts are held on Great Swamp National Wildlife Refuge.

Fortunately, there is also a good deal of public hunting on wildlife-management areas, state forests, and in a few state parks.

The wildlife-management areas are the very heart of public hunting, however. They range in size from 22-acre Amwell Lake Wildlife Management Area to 14,000-acre Peaslee Fish and Widlife Management Area.

Wharton State Forest is also large—99,639 acres—and there are 11,223-acre Belleplain State Forest, and 27,304-acre Lebanon State Forest. State parks on which hunting is permitted include 9,020-acre Wawayanda State Park and 3,112-acre Ringwood State Park. An excellent booklet describing the forests and parks and the facilities available can be obtained from the New Jersey Bureau of Parks, P. O. Box 1420, Trenton, New Jersey 08625.

Information on the wildlife-management areas, including excellent maps of individual areas, can be obtained from the New Jersey Division of Fish, Game, and Shellfisheries, P. O. Box 1809, Trenton, New Jersey 08625.

There is a good deal of hunting on private lands in New Jersey, particularly for birds, deer, and small game in the agricultural areas. The permission of the landowner is needed to hunt such lands, however.

The best white-tailed-deer hunting is found in the northern and western portions of the state. Abram S. Hewitt, Jenny Jump, Norvin Green, Stokes, and Worthington State Forests are good bets. So are Swartswood and Wawayanda State Parks. Good wildlife-management areas, include Peaslee, Stafford Forge, Port Republic, Tuckahoe-Corbin City, Manahawkin, Manchester, Pequest, Millville, Pasadena, Ken Lockwood Gorge, Hamburg Mountain, Hainesville, Greenwood Forest, Glassboro, Flatbrook-Roy, Dennis Creek, Colliers Mills, Clinton, Black River, Turkey Swamp, Wanaque, Wallpack, Whiting, Whittingham, Winslow, Beaver Swamp, and Butterfly Bogs.

The best quail hunting is in the southern counties. Good state forests in this region include Belleplain and Wharton, both sizeable chunks of public hunting land. Wildlife-management areas offering quail hunting include Heislerville, Greenwood Forest, Glassboro, Fortesque, Egg Island-Berrytown, Dix, Dennis, Colliers Mills, Medford, Turkey

There is good bobwhite-quail hunting in southern New Jersey. *Photo by Bob Gooch.*

Swamp, Whiting, Beaver Swamp, Butterfly Bogs, Assunpink, Peaslee, Stafford Forge, Port Republic, Tuckahoe-Corbin, Manahawkin, Manchester, Millville, Nantuxent, Pasadena, and Mad Horse.

Pheasant hunting is reasonably good on Whittingham, Heislerville, Hainesville, Glassboro, Egg Island-Berrytown, Dix, Colliers Mills,

Clinton, Black River, Berkshire Valley, Winslow, Assunpink, Stafford Forge, Port Republic, Tuckahoe-Corbin City, Manahawkin, Nantuxent, and Mad Horse.

The Cape May Country of New Jersey is one of the best woodcock hunting regions in America. The migrating populations build up there, awaiting a favorable tail wind for the long flight across big Delaware Bay. Good wildlife-management areas include Heislerville; Flatbrook-Roy, Dennis Creek, Black River, Turkey Swamp, Wallpack, Whiting, Whittingham, Beaver Swamp, Assunpink, Port Republic, Tuckahoe-Corbin City, and Manahawkin.

While New Jersey is not noted for its grouse, there is some good ruffed-grouse shooting in the state. Good public-hunting areas include the Hamburg Mountain, Hainesville, Greenwood Forest, Glassboro, Flatbrook-Roy, Colliers Mills, Clinton, Black River, Berkshire Valley, Turkey Swamp, Wanaque, Wallpack, Whiting, Whittingham, Winslow, Butterfly Bogs, Peaslee, Ken Lockwood Gorge, Manchester, Pequest, and Pasadena Wildlife Management Areas.

There is good clapper-rail hunting on the Egg Island-Berrytown Fish and Wildlife Management Area.

Cottontail rabbits occur just about statewide, but good Wildlife Management Areas include Egg Island-Berrytown, Dix, Dennis Creek, Heislerville, Peaslee, Stafford Forge, Port Republic, Ken Lockwood Gorge, Tuckahoe-Corbin City, Manahawkin, Manchester, Pequest, Millville, Nantuxent, Pasadena, Mad Horse, Butterfly Bogs, Beaver Swamp, Assunpink, Whiting, Whittingham, Winslow, Wagaque, Wallpack, Turkey Swamp, Berkshire Valley, Colliers Mills, Clinton, Medford, Black River, Hamburg, Hainesville, Greenwood, Glassboro, Fortesque, and Flatbrook-Roy.

Good squirrel hunting Wildlife Management Areas include Port Republic, Ken Lockwood Gorge, Tuckahoe-Corbin City, Manahawkin, Pasadena, Butterfly Bogs, Beaver Swamp, Assunpink, Whiting, Whittingham, Winslow, Wallpack, Turkey Swamp, Berkshire Valley, Colliers Mills, Clinton, Black River, Hamburg, Hainesville, Glassboro, Fortesque, and Flatbrook-Roy.

The fox hunter will find both red and gray foxes on Manchester, Butterfly Bogs, and Egg Island-Berrytown Wildlife Management Areas.

Barnegat Bay, Little Egg Harbor, Great Bay, and Delaware Bay are well-known waterfowling areas in New Jersey, but much of the hunting is on private marshes. There are, however, many good public-hunting areas in New Jersey for both the duck and goose hunter. Among them are Egg Island-Berrytown, Butterfly Bogs, Dix, Dennis Creek, Heislerville, Peaslee, Stafford Forest, Port Republic, Absecon, Tuckahoe-Corbin City, Manahawkin, Millville, Nantuxent, Mad Horse, Beaver Swamp, Assunpink, Whiting, Whittingham, Colliers Mills, Hainesville, Greenwood, Fortesque, and Flatbrook-Roy Wildlife Management Areas.

There is still good hunting in New Jersey.

31 • NEW MEXICO—Desert and Mountain Hunting

A land of mountains, deserts, and plains, New Mexico straddles the Continental Divide and towers upward of twelve thousand feet in the more mountainous regions. Much of the state is arid, but there are also ponderosa pines, green mountains, and lush valleys.

Slightly over one million people live in the 121,666-square-mile Land of Enchantment.

Hunting in New Mexico is varied and interesting. There are both mule and white-tailed deer, antelope, elk, Barbary sheep, cougars, squirrels, turkeys, black bears, bighorn sheep, cottontails and jackrabbits, javelinas, pheasants, quail, prairie chickens, band-tailed pigeons, both mourning and white-winged doves, ducks and geese.

Among the national forests, Bureau of Land Management Lands, and state-owned lands there are an amazing thirty-two million acres of public hunting land. In addition, there are the Indian reservations and millions of acres of private land, most open to hunting on a fee basis.

The national forests include Carson National Forest with headquarters at Taos, NM 87571; Cibola National Forest headquartered at Federal Building, 517 Gold Avenue, S.W., Albuquerque, NM 87101; Gila National Forest at Silver City, NM 88061; Lincoln National Forest at Alamogordo, NM 88310; and Sante Fe National Forest at Sante Fe, NM 87501. Approximately half of the big-game kill in New Mexico comes from these national forest lands. Hunting details and maps can be obtained by writing the forest supervisors at the addresses given.

The fourteen million acres of public land under the jurisdiction of the Bureau of Land Management far exceed the nine million acres of na-

New Mexico produces some trophy mule deer. *Photo by Bob Gooch.*

tional forest lands, and they offer much small-game and bird hunting, as well as hunting for antelope and desert mule deer. Information on the location of these lands and the pertinent hunting regulations are available from the Bureau of Land Management, Box 1449, Albuquerque, New Mexico 87501.

Most Bureau of Reclamation lands are also open to hunting.

Generally, they are adjacent to the major reservoirs. The San Andres National Wildlife Refuge and parts of the Bitter Lake and Bosque de Apache Refuges are open to deer and bighorn-sheep hunting.

Public hunting on the Indian reservations is subject to the approval of the tribes. Information can be obtained by writing the tribal headquarters at Box 147, Dulce, NM 87528, for the Jicarilla Apache Reservation; Mescalero, NM 88340, for the Mescalero Apache Reservation; Window Rock, AZ 86515, for the Navajo Reservations; and Zuni, NM 87327, for the Zuni Reservation.

With nine million acres of leased land under its jurisdiction, the New Mexico Department of Game and Fish matches the national forests for acreage. Full information can be obtained by writing the department at Villagra Building, State Capitol, Sante Fe, New Mexico 87563. An excellent booklet called *Big Game and Turkey Hunting* gives information on these lands, valuable data on other public lands in New Mexico, and information on hunting generally. Among the better wildlife areas are E. S. Barker, Cimarron Canyon, Ed Sargent, Urraca, Bill Humphries, and Marquez.

Parks at Conchas, Elephant Butte, El Vado, Navajo, and Ute Reservoirs are open to big-game and bird hunting.

Sandia Refuge is open for bow hunting, and Big Hatchet Refuge is open for the javelina season.

In addition to the public lands, there is a great deal of private land open to public hunting—either by permission or for a trespass fee.

Both mule and white-tailed deer are found in New Mexico, but the mule deer is the most important big-game species. There are two recognized subspecies, the Rocky Mountain mule deer in the north and the desert mule deer in the south. The best mule-deer hunting is found in the southeast. The Lincoln National Forest and millions of acres of Bureau of Land Management land provide ample hunting territory for all. The Carson National Forest provides the best mule deer hunting in the northwest.

There are also two subspecies of the white-tailed deer, the western whitetail of the southeast and the Coues deer most abundant in the southwest.

The Carson and Sante Fe National Forests in the north offer the best elk hunting, and the plains country of the east provides the best antelope hunting.

There is limited Rocky Mountain bighorn-sheep hunting in the Carson and Santa Fe National Forests, and a limited desert bighorn season in the San Andres Mountains.

Javelina hunting is limited to a few southwestern counties. There is also limited hunting for such exotic game as gemsbok, Barbary sheep, and ibex. Black bears are found in most of the national forests, and cougars are hunted in the northeast and southeast portions of New Mexico.

Fall and spring turkey hunting is permitted in most areas where the big birds are found—generally the northeastern and southwestern parts of the state. Three subspecies are present, the Merriam's—the most abundant—the Rio Grande, and a Mexican species which is fully protected. The Gila and Cibola National Forests offer good turkey-hunting.

Three quail—scaled, Gambel's, and the bobwhite—top the list of game birds in arid New Mexico. The scaled is the most abundant and the most widely distributed. These popular birds are plentiful in the eastern and southern parts of the state, and finding a place to hunt them is rarely a problem. The Gambel's is found primarily in the central and southwestern regions, particularly along the streams. The bobwhite is limited to a few eastern counties. New Mexico is on the western fringe of the prime bobwhite range.

There is limited white-winged dove hunting in the southwest, but the best mourning-dove shooting is in the eastern counties and the lower Rio Grande Valley. The mourning-dove kill far exceeds that off the whitewing.

Blue grouse and the lesser prairie chicken represent the family so far as huntable populations of grouse go. Both are limited, however. Blue grouse are found in the higher mountains, and prairie chickens are hunted in a few eastern counties. Pheasant hunting is limited to a brief season in December.

The Rio Grande and Pecos Valleys support the bulk of the waterfowl hunting. The Pecos River near Roswell offers interesting shooting for lesser sandhill cranes.

Both cottontails and jackrabbits are abundant in New Mexico and occur just about statewide. The handsome Albert, or tassel-eared, squirrel is popular among some hunters. They are hunted primarily in the ponderosa pines of the southwest.

Hunting in New Mexico—like the land—is enchanting.

32 • NEW YORK—Eastern Big Game

Metropolitan in the minds of many, New York is an interesting region of sea coasts, rolling hills, and rugged mountains. Almost twenty million people live in its varied 49,576 square miles.

New York is among the top eastern white-tailed deer states, and except for Maine, it has the largest black-bear population east of the Mississippi. The state also has good wild-turkey hunting, making it one of the best big-game states in the East.

The annual pheasant harvest will run well in excess of 300,000 birds in good years, but the ruffed grouse is also an important game bird. There is limited bobwhite-quail hunting on Long Island, but the woodcock is of more interest to most wing shots. Snipes and rails complete the game bird picture in the Empire state.

The cottontail rabbit is the most popular small-game animal, but snowshoe hares are also abundant in the major forest areas. Grays dominate the squirrel populations, and they are abundant and popular among small-game hunters. There are also a few fox squirrels. There is an abundance of raccoons for the state's enthusiastic night hunters. Woodchucks are abundant, and there are also bobcats, coyotes, and red and gray foxes. European hares have been introduced and provide exotic, though limited, hunting in some regions.

The waterfowl hunting is fair along Long Island Sound, the Great Lakes, on many inland lakes, and along numerous streams.

There are no major federal hunting lands in New York, but there is really no need for them, with state lands providing an estimated three and one-half million acres. Some hunting is permitted on Whitney Point

Reservoir and Moose River Recreation Areas, Hector Grazing Cooperative Area, Montezuma National Wildlife Refuge, and Iroquois National Wildlife Refuge, however. All are federal areas. Hunting information is available from the New York State Department of Environmental Conservation, Division of Fish and Wildlife, 50 Wolf Road, Albany, New York 12233.

The truly big areas are the famous Adirondack and Catskill State Forest Preserves, totaling a bit more than two and one-half million acres. State parks, forty Fish and Wildlife Management Act Cooperative Hunting Areas, thirty-nine wildlife-management areas, and state forests make up the bulk of the remaining million-odd acres. Information on these areas can be obtained from the Department of Environmental Conservation. Also available from the Department of Environmental Conservation are brochures of the wildlife-management areas and Fish and Wildlife Management Act Cooperative Areas, as well as county maps showing all public hunting lands. The maps sell for fifty cents each.

There is much good hunting on private lands in the state, but the permission of the landowner is needed before entering such lands to hunt. The cooperative-hunting areas are actually on private land, and special permits are needed to hunt some of them.

The deer hunter will experience little trouble finding a place to hunt, though much land is posted. Both the Adirondack and Catskill Forest Preserves support public hunting for whitetails, but they are not highly productive areas. The counties of Allegany, Cattaraugus, Delaware, Steuben, and Sullivan produce high deer harvests.

The Adirondack Forest Preserve supports the bulk of the bear hunting, though the Catskill Preserve is usually good also. The Catskills are not always open to bear hunting, however.

Turkey hunting, a fast growing form of hunting in New York, is best in Allegany, Cattaraugus, Delaware, Steuben and Sullivan Counties. There are public hunting lands in these counties.

The best pheasant hunting is on the private farms of the Lake Plains and Finger Lakes Regions. Cayuga, Livingston, and Seneca Counties are good, and there are public hunting areas worth investigating.

The southern tier counties, also noted for their deer hunting, are the heart of grouse hunting in New York. The periphery of the Adirondack and Catskill Forest Preserve is also good. These areas are so vast and productive of grouse that there is little reason for the hunter to look elsewhere.

The only quail hunting in New York is on Long Island, where the

The cottontail rabbit is the most popular small-game animal in New York. *Photo by New York Division of Fish and Wildlife.*

Suffolk County Fish and Wildlife Management Cooperative Area offers good public hunting.

The Hungarian partridge is limited to Jefferson and St. Lawrence Counties, but seasons are held sporadically.

The marshes of Lakes Erie and Ontario and Long Island offer fair snipe and rail hunting, and the fringe areas of the large forest preserves offer good woodcock hunting.

The cottontail rabbit in New York, as it is everywhere, is a product of the farming community, and the best hunting is found on private lands. However, just about all of the wildlife-management areas and the Fish and Wildlife Management Act Cooperative Areas offer cottontail hunting. The Adirondack Forest Preserve is an excellent bet for snowshoe hares, as are the other northern public hunting lands on which spruce is the predominant forest cover.

The European hare may be found in very limited numbers in northern Schoharie and southern Montgomery Counties.

Gray squirrels will be found on just about all of the forested public hunting lands of the state with the exception of the Adirondack Forest Preserve. Fox squirrels are limited to the western part of the state, however, and are not really abundant there. Possibly the best squirrel hunting in the state can be found in the southern tier counties—much of the best on private lands.

Raccoons roam just about all of the public hunting lands in New York, but the hunting is generally best in the agricultural counties. Foxes and woodchucks are also abundant in the farming country. Bobcats and coyotes are fairly abundant in the Adirondack Forest Preserve.

That's the hunting picture in New York state—varied, interesting, and usually productive.

33 • NORTH CAROLINA—For Hunting Variety

North Carolina's varied terrain offers hunting to suit the tastes of just about any big-game, small-game, wing-shooting, or waterfowl hunter. The state's interesting country ranges from the almost barren Outer Banks to the lofty Great Smoky Mountains. In between there are a wide variety of marshes, rolling hills, flat coastal lands, and rugged mountains and foothills.

Over five million people live in the state's 52,712 square miles.

North Carolina has a rapidly growing white-tailed deer herd, and limited black-bear and turkey hunting. It is also one of the few states that offers hunting for wild boar.

The bird hunter will find good hunting for both grouse and bobwhite quail, but the grouse hunting is physically demanding, as is typical of grouse hunting in the Southern Appalachians. A small population of ring-necked pheasants inhabits Hatteras Island on the Outer Banks, but they are not hunted. The mourning-dove hunting is excellent, and the annual harvest runs into several million birds. There are reasonably good winter populations of snipes and woodcocks, and rails are abundant along the coast. The clapper is the most popular, but there are also sora and king rails in the freshwater marshes.

Cottontail rabbits are abundant, and there are swamp rabbits in the Tidewater Region. Gray squirrels are also plentiful, and there are a few fox squirrels in isolated areas. An abundance of raccoons and opossums in the Piedmont and Coastal Plains, red and gray foxes, and woodchucks round out the small-game offering.

The North Carolina coast, including the famous Currituck Sound, offers some of the finest waterfowl hunting in America.

With 1,125,196 acres of national forests in North Carolina, federal lands are abundant. The national forests include 150,000-acre Croatan, 449,281-acre Nantahala, 478,297-acre Pisgah, and 43,571-acre Uwharrie. Hunting information and maps are available from the Forest Supervisor, National Forests in North Carolina, U.S. Forest Service, Box 731, Asheville, North Carolina 28802. There is some goose and duck hunting adjacent to the Mattamuskeet National Wildlife Refuge, and the North Carolina Wildlife Resources Commission, Albemarle Building, 325 North Salisbury Street, Raleigh, North Carolina 27611, can supply the details. Or write the Refuge Manager, Lake Mattamuskeet National Wildlife Refuge, New Holland, North Carolina 27885.

There is also some waterfowl-hunting on the Cape Hatteras National Seashore Park. The Park Superintendent, National Park Service, Manteo, North Carolina 27954, can advise on this hunting.

Finally, there is some public hunting on the lands of the U.S. Army Corps of Engineers and the various military reservations. Write the Wildlife Resources Commission for details.

While the federal lands support much excellent hunting, the North Carolina game lands are the very heart of public hunting in the state. These well-managed lands now approach two million acres and are continuing to grow. Many are on federal lands, the lands of other state agencies, and on the lands of timber companies and other private owners. There are over a hundred game lands, ranging in size from 100-acre White Oak River Impoundment Game Land in Onslow County to 178,014-acre Dare Game Land on First Colony Farms in Dare County.

There is also some public hunting on Indian reservations, and information is available from the Wildlife Resources Commission.

Numerous corporations open their lands to public hunting, much of it in the form of game lands managed by the Wildlife Resources Commission. Among them are Rand-Dale Farms, Inc., Albemarle Paper Company, Champion International, Catawba Paper Company, International Paper Company, Duke Power Company, and the Weyerhauser Company.

There is much excellent hunting on private lands, particularly in the extensive farming community. The permission of the landowner is required, however.

The white-tailed deer is North Carolina's most important big game animal, and many of the game lands offer good deer hunting. Among them are Chowan Swamp, Croatan, Dismal Swamp, First Colony,

The bobwhite quail is king in North Carolina. *Courtesy of Luther Partin.*

Goshen, Goose Creek, Nantahala, Pisgah, Sandhills, Uwharrie, and White Oak Swamp.

With the Great Smoky Mountain National Park a major bear sanctuary, the western game lands offer the best black-bear hunting. Good ones include Nantahala, Pisgah, and Toxaway, but there is good bear hunting in the eastern swamps also. There the Angola Bay, Croatan, Goose Creek, and Lukens Island Game Lands offer bear hunting. Wild boar hunting is pretty much limited to the Nantahala Game Lands in the extreme western part of the state.

The wild turkey is just starting to make a comeback in North Carolina, and hunting is now limited to the spring gobbler season only. Game lands include Caswell, Croatan, Green River, New Hope, Pisgah, Robbins, and Sandhills.

Quail are found in just about every county in the state. The best hunting is usually on farmlands, but there are over forty game lands offering bobwhite hunting. Among them are Caswell, Corinth, Croatan, Dare, Embro, Fork Creek, Huntsville Penderlea, Scuppernog, and Spruill Farms.

Good dove game lands are also abundant, including Brownstown Farms, Dysartsville, New Hope, Nutbush Peninsula, and Sandhills. Like quail, however, the best dove-hunting is found often on farmlands, particularly on those on which grain is a major crop.

The ruffed grouse is found only in the western mountains, but there are some prime game lands including Cherokee, Nantahala, Pisgah, and Thurmond Chatham.

Woodcocks occur primarily in the coastal plains where the Chowan, Scuppernog, and Spruill Farms Game Lands are possibilities. The Northwest River Marsh, North River and other coastal game lands are good bets for rails.

There are over fifty game lands offering hunting for gray squirrels, and fox squirrels are found on Sandhills. Good areas for grays include Bluff Mountain, Carson Woods, Cherokee, Chowan Swamp, Holly Shelter, Lukens Island, Nantahala, South Mountains, Uwharrie, and White Oak Swamp, among many others.

Rabbits, too, are found statewide. Dare, Dismal Swamp, Goose Creek, Gull Rock, Lick Skillet, New Hope, Penderlea, and River View are among the better rabbit game lands. Raccoons, opossums, and woodchucks are found just about statewide, with the raccoon most abundant in the east and chucks plentiful in the northwestern pastures.

Catfish Lake, Chowan Swamp, Croatan, Dare, First Colony, Goose Creek, Gull Rock, Jarret Bay, Lukens Island, North River, Northwest River, Scuppernong, Smith Creek, Swan Lake, and White Oak River Game Lands offer good waterfowl hunting, but commercial guides in the Currituck Sound and Lake Mattamuskeet regions are the best bet for a rare waterfowl hunt.

Hunting is good in the Tarheel State.

34 • NORTH DAKOTA—A Game-Bird State

North Dakota claims 70,665 square miles of America's rolling prairie, most relatively flat, though White Butte in the southwestern badlands stretches to 3,506 feet. Over 100,000 of its estimated 700,000 people hunt, recording such impressive bags as 150,000 sharp-tailed grouse, 400,000 ducks, and 100,000 geese during most seasons.

The big plains state is a bird hunter's paradise, offering such exciting species as sharp-tailed and ruffed grouse, Hungarian partridge, pheasants, sage grouse, ducks, geese, sandhill cranes, snipes and coots.

The waterfowl hunting rates with the best in the nation, but the sharp-tailed-grouse hunting could well be the best on the continent. Pinnated grouse and chukar partridge are present, but not in huntable numbers. Doves are abundant, but seasons are not held every year.

The small-game hunter will find an abundance of rabbits—cottontails, jacks, and some snowshoes—plus limited fox- and gray-squirrel hunting.

Big game includes both mule and white-tailed deer, antelope, wild turkeys, moose, and bighorn sheep. Moose, antelope, and wild turkeys are limited to residents, but nonresidents may hunt antelope with a bow. The bighorn-sheep and moose hunting is extremely limited, with only a dozen permits issued each season.

Coyotes and foxes round out a varied list of eligible game species.

The best sharp-tailed-grouse hunting is found west of U. S. Highway 85 and primarily in the counties of Slope, Golden Valley, and Billings, counties in which there is a good deal of public hunting in the national grasslands.

The prime waterfowl hunting is in the famous North Dakota pothole country of the east. State game- and fish-management areas and waterfowl-production areas offer almost unlimited hunting territory.

While federal lands are limited in North Dakota, the Little Missouri Grasslands and the Custer National Forest offer over a million acres of hunting in the extreme western part of the state. This is prime sharp-tailed grouse, mule and white-tailed deer, and antelope country. Complete information and maps are available from the U.S. Department of Agriculture, Custer National Forest, P. O. Box 2556, Billings, Montana 59103. District Rangers are located at Dickinson, North Dakota 58601, and Wafford City, North Dakota 58854.

Grassland units along the North Dakota-South Dakota border include Grand River and Cedar River with headquarters at Box 390, Lemmon, South Dakota 57638, and Sheyenne, headquartered at Lisbon, North Dakota 58054. Sheyenne offers white-tailed deer, small game, and waterfowl.

There are also limited public lands owned by the Bureau of Land Management and the U.S. Army Corps of Engineers. The Corps of Engineers lands border the big reservoirs along the Missouri River.

The waterfowler can choose from an estimated three-hundred waterfowl-production areas administered by the U.S. Fish and Wildlife Service. They provide hunting for small game and white-tailed deer, as well as hunting for ducks and geese. A location map of these areas can be obtained from the North Dakota office of the U.S. Fish and Wildlife Service, Box 1897, Bismarck, North Dakota 58501. There is no cost.

The North Dakota Game and Fish Department owns 136 excellent Game and Fish Management Areas that, collectively, offer hunting for just about any kind of game in the state. They range in size from one-acre Red River Access Management Area in Pembina County to 11,285-acre Audubon Game Management Area in McLean County. Hunting is prohibited on a few reserved as havens for strugging species, such as pinnated grouse, but the great majority are open. Many are large, in the 1,000- to 6,000-acre range. An excellent brochure on these game-management areas can be obtained by writing the North Dakota Game and Fish Department, 2121 Lovett Avenue, Bismarck, North Dakota 58505. The brochure includes a location map and detailed descriptions of the kind of hunting available on each.

While public-hunting land is reasonably abundant in North Dakota, assuring resident and nonresident alike of a place to hunt, the bulk of the state's lands are privately owned. Approximately 95 percent of the state is composed of farms and ranches, but obtaining permission to hunt most of them is not difficult.

North Dakota is one of our top sharp-tailed grouse states. *Photo by Bob Gooch.*

North Dakota's posting and trespass law is reasonable. It is unlawful to hunt on lands legally posted without first obtaining permission from the owner *or* tenant. Owners may be hard to locate, but tenants seldom are. *Legal posting* means signs stating "Hunting Is Not Permitted." They must bear the name and address of the owner or tenant and state the date of posting. On unfenced property, the signs must be posted every 440 yards, but on the gates only of fenced property. Even if the land is not posted, it is illegal to hunt, without the owner's permission, fields of alfalfa, clover, and other grasses grown for seed.

It is also unlawful to hunt within 440 yards of occupied buildings or residences without the owner's consent.

There are thousands of acres of unposted private lands in North Dakota, lands I have personally hunted successfully for both sharp-tailed grouse and Hungarian partridge.

Dakota is an Indian word meaning "allies or friends," and the North Dakotans live up to this image. The overworked staff of the Game and Fish Department is friendly and helpful, and the citizens of the state are equally so. Hunting pressure is light, and the people harbor no ill will toward the sportsmen who come to their state for the fine hunting.

The hunter can turn to North Dakota for some of the finest sharp-tailed grouse hunting to be found anywhere. Particularly good are the fringe areas between the farmlands and the famous North Dakota Badlands of the southwest. Here the natives hunt the "breaks," the marginal edges between the grain fields and the rough stuff. The birds feed on the lush farms but seek the badlands for cover and protection.

The Hungarian-partridge hunting is also superb, but most of it is found on the big grain farms and ranches. Huns occur all over the state.

The state's fine waterfowl is the only game that has been subjected to heavy hunting pressure in recent years. In order to ease it, nonresidents are limited to ten consecutive days and restricted to selected hunting zones. The eastern half of the state is most productive for waterfowl.

The sharptails, Huns, and waterfowl make North Dakota a top game-bird state. They can also make a trip to the Flickertail State well worthwhile.

35 • OHIO—For Trophy Deer

Big and heavily populated, Ohio's 41,222 square miles is home to eleven million Americans, many of them avid hunters. Good game management has been successful in maintaining good hunting under the very heels of civilization.

Good deer hunting, and fair turkey hunting during the spring season only, is the big-game picture in Ohio. Ohio white-tailed-deer hunters bag some of the largest deer in America, and the success ratio of Ohio hunters is better than those in Michigan and Pennsylvania.

Fair pheasant hunting in limited areas, good ruffed-grouse hunting in some regions, good bobwhite-quail, woodcock, rail and snipe hunting along the Lake Erie marshes offer interesting hunting for the wing shot.

Probably the most fortunate of the Ohio hunters are the small-game men who go after rabbits and squirrels. The cottontail rabbit is the number one game species in the big Midwestern state, and both fox and gray squirrels are abundant. An abundance of raccoons and opossums, foxes and woodchucks, round out the small-game list in the state.

With many miles of water frontage along Lake Erie and many inland streams, Ohio has long been a fair waterfowl state. While its best waterfowling is now history, there is still good hunting, though much of it is on privately-owned marshes.

The Wayne National Forest in the southeastern part of the state is the major federal land in Ohio. It offers 106,129 acres of public hunting land. A map of the forest, plus hunting information, can be obtained from ranger stations at Ironton, Ohio 45638, and Athens, Ohio 45701. There is also limited hunting on U. S. Army Corps of Engineers lands, Bureau of Reclamation lands, and military reservations. Information on these areas can be obtained by writing the Ohio Division of Wildlife, Department of Natural Resources, 1500 Dublin Road, Columbus, Ohio 43212.

The Ohio Division of Wildlife Management Areas and state forests are the very heart of public hunting in the state, however. There is also some public hunting in the state parks. Many of these areas are small—just a few acres—but some run big—over fifty thousand acres. For example, the Miltonville Access Area is only one acre, but the Shawnee State Forest is a sprawling 58,000-acre area. The Division of Wildlife maintains an inventory of all public hunting lands in the state—federal, state, local, and private—and this information is available for the asking. available for the asking.

Private lands support a good deal of public hunting in Ohio. A major landowner is the Ohio Power Company, P. O. Box 328, McConnelsville, Ohio 43756. Hunting is permitted on much of the company's forty-four thousand acres upon written request to the company.

The Ohio Wildlife Cooperative Hunting Program has opened up thousands of acres of private land to public hunting. Initiated by the Division of Wildlife, it gives control of hunting to the landowner and provides him with the necessary signs and other materials needed to make the program work.

The hill country of eastern and southeastern Ohio offers the best deer hunting. Some good public-hunting areas include 4,000-acre Perry County Reclamation Area, 10,586-acre Pike Lake State Park and Forest, Scioto Trail State Forest and Park, Tar Hollow State Forest and Park, Zaleski State Forest, Avon Wildlife Area, Blue Rock State Forest and Park, Cooper Hollow Wildlife Area, Hocking State Forest, and Mead Wildlife Area. The Wayne National Forest is also a good choice for the deer hunter. The turkey hunter will find the best hunting in Hocking, Pike, and Vinton Counties.

Central Ohio offers the best pheasant hunting. Good public-hunting areas include the Willard Marsh Wildlife Area, Kelleys Island, Killdeer Plains and Wildlife Area, and Little Portage Wildlife Area. The best pheasant hunting is likely on private lands, however. Grouse are most abundant in the southeastern and northeastern parts of the state. Good public-hunting areas include big Wayne National Forest, Shawnee State Forest, Hocking State Forest, and Waterloo State Forest.

While Ohio is the northern extreme of the bobwhite quail's range, the birds are found just about all over the state with the best hunting on private farmlands. The birds are abundant in the southern half of the state, however. The cooperative hunting areas should be good. Big Island Wildlife Area, Brush Creek State Forest, Rocky Fork Lake State Park, and Tycoon Lake Wildlife Area are among the best public-hunting areas.

Heavily-populated Ohio produces some trophy white-tailed deer. *Photo by Ohio Division of Wildlife.*

The Little Portage Wildlife Area should be good for snipe hunting, and Pymatuning State Park, Orwell Wildlife Area, and Metzger Marsh Wildlife Area are among the better public hunting areas for woodcocks.

With both fox and gray squirrels abundant in the state, there is almost unlimited public hunting for these popular little animals. The Wayne National Forest is a good choice. Most of the state forests are also good. Try Blue Rock, Brush Creek, Dean, Fernwood, Hocking, Maumee, Pike Lake, Scioto Trail, Shade River, Shawnee, Tar Hollow, Waterloo, and Zaleski. Many of the state parks are also good. Just about any public hunting area with a good stand of hardwoods is a possibility for the squirrel hunter.

Ohio's annual harvest of cottontail rabbits exceeds two million. The popular game animals are found all over Ohio, but the best hunting is in the hill country of the southeastern part of the state. Good public-hunting areas include Atwood Reservoir, Avondale Wildlife Area, Berlin Reservoir Wildlife Area, Powelson Wildlife Area, Tappan Reservoir, Wolf Creek Wildlife Area, and Wolf Run State Park. Actually, a complete list of the rabbit-hunting possibilities is too lengthy to include here.

Raccoons, too, are found all over the state, and just about any public hunting area is a good possibility. Wooded areas near streams, marshes, and lakes are usually good coon habitat.

Atwood Reservoir, Bolivar Dry Dam, and Brush Creek Wildlife Area offer good woodchuck hunting, but the best of the hunting will be found on private lands.

While the best waterfowl hunting occurs on privately owned marshes, there is reasonably good hunting on the public hunting areas. Included among the better ones are Portage Lake State Park, Beach City Reservoir, Buckeye Lake State Park, Burr Oak Lake State Park, Kiser Lake State Park, Lake Loramie, Grand Lake, St. Marys State Park, Metzger Marsh Wildlife Area, Magee Marsh Wildlife Area, Killdeer Wildlife Area, and Mosquito Creek Reservoir Wildlife Area.

There is good hunting in crowded Ohio—for the hunter who is willing to work for it.

36 • OKLAHOMA—For Prairie Chickens

Ranging in elevation from four hundred feet in the east to four thousand in the west, Oklahoma is a state of varied terrain and rich game lands. Slightly less than three million people occupy its 69,919 square miles. The hunting population is approximately 15 percent of the total population.

The quail is Oklahoma's top game-bird, and the birds are the leading game crop in the big plains state. Most are bobwhites, but there is some scaled-quail hunting in the west. The mourning dove hunting is excellent, and Oklahoma is the only state in the nation offering both greater and lesser prairie chickens. Ring-necked pheasants, snipes, rails, and woodcocks round out the bird hunting.

The white-tailed deer is found statewide, and there are a few mule deer in the west. Wild turkeys are plentiful in the western half of the state, and there is very limited antelope and elk hunting.

Cottontails, swamp rabbits, and jackrabbits plus fox and gray squirrels are the major small-game animals, and there are raccoons for the night hunter.

Rivers, creeks, farm ponds, and numerous large impoundments offer good waterfowl hunting for ducks, geese, and even sandhill cranes.

Federal lands in Oklahoma are as varied as the terrain and offer many acres of excellent hunting, much of it under cooperative agreements with the Oklahoma Department of Wildlife Conservation.

The Ouachita National Forest provides approximately 200,000 acres of hunting land in the southeastern corner of the state. Headquarters for maps and hunting information is located at Hot Springs, Arkansas 71901.

Probably more important to bird hunters are the Rita Blanca and Black Kettle National Grasslands, both near the Texas border. These grasslands are also administered by the U.S. Forest Service with headquarters at 517 Gold Avenue, S.W., Albuquerque, New Mexico 87101. There is also a wide variety of good hunting available on the U.S. Army Corps of Engineers lands, much of it under the supervision of the Oklahoma Department of Wildlife Conservation. The Department has information on these public hunting lands, and the Corps of Engineers can be contacted at Box 61, Tulsa, Oklahoma 74101.

Another Federal agency with large land holdings in Oklahoma is the U.S. Bureau of Reclamation, Federal Courthouse Building, Oklahoma City, Oklahoma 73125.

This land is also available for public hunting under the supervision of the Department of Wildlife Conservation.

Finally, there is the Wichita Mountains Wildlife Refuge under the direction of the U.S. Fish and Wildlife Service, Federal Courthouse Building, Oklahoma City, Oklahoma 73125.

In addition to the federal lands it manages for public hunting, the Oklahoma Department of Wildlife Conservation, 1801 North Lincoln, Oklahoma City, Oklahoma 73105, owns outright many acres of game lands offering hunting for just about every species found in the state. Among them are 13,640-acre Cookson Hills Game Management Area, on which special deer hunts are held; 3,876-acre Ellis County Public Hunting Area; 9,273-acre Lexington Public Hunting Area; 8,154-acre Okmulgee Public Hunting Area; and 2,260-acre Stringtown Public Hunting Area.

On some areas, hunting is limited to special hunts, but on others there are no restrictions other than the general hunting regulations. Full information on these fine hunting-lands is contained in an attractive booklet called *Public Hunting Lands of Oklahoma.* It is available for fifty cents to cover postage and handling.

While public hunting is good in Oklahoma, an estimated 95 percent of the state is privately owned, and such land supports the bulk of the hunting.

Hunting pressure is not heavy in Oklahoma, and obtaining permission to hunt on private lands is not difficult, though it is becoming increasingly difficult near the major cities.

The posting law in Oklahoma is simple. The hunter must have the landowner's permission, but written permission is not required. Unoccupied land is open to hunting without permission, however.

There are an estimated 850,000 acres of land in commercial forests

Pointing dogs are popular in Oklahoma where the bobwhite quail is the leading game bird. *Photo by Oklahoma Department of Wildlife Conservation.*

where hunting is usually permitted. The names of these owners, mostly corporations, are available from the Department of Wildlife Conservation.

The quail, the number one game species in Oklahoma, is found all over the state. The best hunting generally occurs in the western part of the state, but there is much good hunting in the eastern farming area. The Rita Blanca National Grasslands is a good bet for scaled quail, a bird limited to the far western part of Oklahoma. While the best bobwhite hunting will most likely be found on private land, good public hunting areas include Altus-Lugert, Arbuckle, Black Kettle, Canton, Ellis County, Fort Supply, Lexington, Oologah, Pine Creek, and Tishomingo Public Hunting Areas.

The best prairie chicken hunting occurs in Osage County. The Osage Public Hunting Area is managed primarily for the greater prairie chicken. Ellis County Public Hunting Area also holds some prairie chickens.

Doves are found throughout the state with the best hunting in private farming areas. There is also good dove hunting on the Altus-Lugert, Black Kettle, Canton, Ellis County, Fort Cobb, Fort Supply, Gruber, Hulah, Keyston, Lexington, and Love Valley Public Hunting Areas.

The best pheasant hunting is located in the Panhandle Counties, and usually on private land.

While white-tailed deer are found in all of Oklahoma's seventy-seven counties, the southeast offers the best hunting. The Ouchita National Forest provides good deer hunting as do the Broken Bow Lake, Chouteau, Fort Supply, Gruber, and Stringtown Public Hunting Areas. The top deer counties are Cherokee, Delaware, LeFlore, McCurtain, Osage, and Pittsburg.

The state's excellent wild-turkey hunting is best in the western river drainages. The Black Kettle, Canton, and Ellis County Public Hunting Areas are good.

Finally, there is good waterfowl-hunting on the Fort Gibson, Hulah, and Wister Public Hunting Areas. There is also great hunting on the Great Salt Plains, R. S. Kerr, Sequoyah, and Tishomingo National Wildlife Refuges, rounding out a rich variety of Oklahoma hunting.

37 • OREGON—For Antelope, Deer, Elk, and Birds

Laced by rushing streams, dotted by sparkling lakes, and stunningly scenic, Oregon is truly a hunter's paradise. Slightly over two million people live in its ninety-seven thousand square miles.

The big-game offering is varied—an abundance of mule deer, Columbian black-tailed deer, a few white-tailed deer, antelope, Rocky Mountain and Roosevelt elk, an abundance of black bears, a few bighorn sheep, a few mountain goats, and cougars. There is no season on the mountain goats.

The bird hunter will be pleased with the pheasant hunting, but there are also mourning doves, band-tailed pigeons, chukar partridge, Hungarian partridge; valley, mountain, and bobwhite quail; blue, ruffed, and sage grouse; wild turkeys, and snipes. Bobwhite quail are almost nonexistent, however.

The small-game hunter can choose among snowshoe rabbits, black-tailed and white-tailed jacks, cottontails, and brush rabbits. The western gray is the primary game-squirrel, though there are also introduced gray and fox squirrels in isolated areas. Additional animals are rockchucks, coyotes, and bobcats.

Oregon is also a top waterfowl state. Many ducks and geese breed in the state, but many more migrate into Oregon from higher latitudes. Black brant are an interesting addition to the usual variety of ducks and geese found along the Pacific coast.

With fifty percent of Oregon's ninety-seven thousand square miles in public ownership, there is no problem finding a place to hunt.

Thirteen national forests offer an estimated 12 million acres of fine public hunting land. They are Suislaw National Forest with 600,000 acres, headquartered at Corvallis, OR 97330; Mt. Hood and over 1 million acres of land, headquartered at Portland, OR 97208; Williamette National Forest with 1.5 million acres, headquartered at Eugene, OR 97401; Deschutes with another 1.5 million acres, headquartered at Bend, OR 97701; Ochoco with an estimated 850,000 acres, headquartered at Prineville, OR 97754; Umatilla National Forest, one million acres, headquartered at Pendleton, OR 97801; Wallowa-Whitman National Forest with 2.25 million acres, headquartered at Baker, OR 97814; Malheur with 1.5 million acres, headquartered at John Day, OR 97845; Umpqua National Forest with nearly a million acres, headquartered at Roseburg, OR 97470; Rogue with over 800,000 acres, headquartered at Medford, OR 97501; Winema National Forest with 900,000 acres, headquartered at Klamath Falls, OR 97601; Fremont National Forest with 1.25 million acres, headquartered at Lakeview, OR 97630; and Siskiyou National Forest with over a million acres, headquartered at Grants Pass, OR 97526.

Write the forest supervisors at the headquarters of the respective forests for maps and hunting information—or write the U.S. Forest Service, P.O. Box 3623, Portland, Oregon 97208.

The Bureau of Land Management owns an estimated 75 percent of the southeast quarter of Oregon. This Federal agency also owns big chunks of good hunting land in the west near the coast and in the north-central part of the state. For complete information on these vast federal lands, write the Bureau of Land Management, U.S. Department of the Interior, 729 N.E. Oregon Street, P.O. Box 3861, Portland Oregon 97208. Also ask for the excellent *BLM Recreation Guide*, a map and guide showing the location of most public lands in Oregon. This map can become an invaluable tool for locating good hunting territory.

Other federal lands include national wildlife refuges, U.S. Army Corps of Engineers Lands, and Bureau of Reclamation lands. Write the Oregon Department of Fish and Wildlife, P.O. Box 3503, Portland, Oregon 97208, for information on hunting these lands.

The Oregon Department of Fish and Wildlife owns 110,000 acres of land in seventeen Wildlife Areas. Information on these lands is available from the Department.

Private corporations own thousands of acres of land that is open to public hunting. Leading companies are members of the American Forest Products Industries, 1835 K Street NW, Washington, D.C. 20006. Write there for information.

Hunting on cultivated or enclosed private lands without the consent of the landowner is illegal.

Oregon hunters enjoy fine mule-deer hunting. *Courtesy of Oregon Department of Fish and Wildlife.*

Every county in central Oregon provides good mule-deer hunting. Southeastern Oregon is also good, and muleys are numerous through the Blue and Wallowa Mountains of northeast Oregon. Tillamook and Coos Counties along the coast are good for black-tailed deer, and Lane and Linn Counties on the west slope of Cascades are also good.

Rocky Mountain elk range the rugged mountains in the eastern part of the state, and Roosevelt elk live in the Coast and Cascade Mountains. Wallowa, Union, Grant, Morrow, and Baker Counties are tops for Rocky Mountain elk. Roosevelt elk are most abundant in Clatsop and Tillamook Counties on the north coast. The Coos and Coquille River Drainages are good in the south.

Antelope are found among the sagebrush flats of southeastern Oregon. Good counties include Crook, Deschutes, Lake, Harney, and Malheur.

Black bears are found just about statewide, but the Saddle Mountain, Big Creel, and Cannon Beach areas in Clatsop County are particularly good.

The pheasant hunting is best in the grain areas east of the Cascades, and Malheur County is a top area. The wheatlands of the Columbia Basin are also good.

Chukar partridge are abundant in eastern Oregon, and are most abundant in the lower portions of the Deschutes, John Day, and Snake River Drainages. Hungarian partridge are found primarily in northeastern Oregon.

The Umpqua and Willamette Valleys support good valley-quail populations, but these birds are found statewide in suitable habitat. The same is true of the mountain quail, but the birds are most numerous in the Coast, Cascade, Blue, and Wallowa Mountains.

The Blue and Wallowa Mountains and the west slope of the Cascades are good for blue grouse. Ruffed grouse are found primarily in willow and alder thickets. Western Oregon is good. Lake, Harney, and Malheur Counties in the southeast support fair sage-grouse populations, but they are not hunted every year.

Waterfowl are found in all lowland marshes and water areas of the state. Generally, the early hunting is best in Klamath, Lake, and Harney Counties. The peak of the migration offers good hunting along the Snake River. The best mallard-shooting is found along the Snake River and in the Willamette Valley. Grain fields in Umatilla, Morrow, Gillam, and Sherman Counties offer good goose shooting.

Rabbits of one kind or another range the state. The snowshoes are limited to the higher elevations and timbered country. The black-tailed jack is the most abundant east of the Cascades in the sagebrush country. There is often an abundance of western gray squirrels in the northern part of Willamette Valley.

The Oregon hunter does not lack for an abundance of game.

38 • PENNSYLVANIA—Deer, Grouse, Pheasants, and Turkeys

Boasting the largest white-tailed deer harvest in the East, one of the largest wild turkey populations, and a ring-necked pheasant harvest in excess of a million birds, Pennsylvania is truly a hunter's paradise. The ruffed-grouse hunting is also tops. Almost twelve million people, many of them hunters, live in the state's 45,333 square miles.

The Pennsylvania big-game hunter enjoys some of the best white-tailed deer hunting in America, and the wild turkey hunting is of equal quality. The bear harvest is modest, but good by eastern standards. Bear seasons are not held every year.

The bird hunter will find that Pennsylvania has some of the best pheasant hunting in America, a fact not generally recognized. The ruffed-grouse hunting is good, but spotty. There is also some fine woodcock hunting in the state, plus limited bobwhite-quail, snipe, and rail hunting.

The small-game hunter will find both fox and gray squirrels. There is also an abundance of cottontail rabbits and a few snowshoe hares. Raccoons are very abundant, and night hunting is popular. Foxes are also found statewide and are hunted by a variety of methods. The woodchuck hunting is excellent, and some chucks can be found in just about every county.

While Pennsylvania is not among the top waterfowl states, there is good hunting for both ducks and geese. Waterfowl hunting tends to be spotty in the state—good in some regions, almost nonexistent in others.

While federal lands are somewhat limited in Pennsylvania, various state lands offer almost unlimited public-hunting possibilities.

Pennsylvania has the largest white-tailed deer harvest in the East. *Photo by Pennsylvania Game Commission.*

The major federal land in Pennsylvania is 471,081-acre Allegheny National Forest, and hunting information and maps can be obtained from the Forest Supervisor, Allegheny National Forest, P.O. Box 847, Warren, Pennsylvania 16365. Other Federal lands are extremely limited, but the Pennsylvania Game Commission, P.O. Box 1567, Harrisburg, Pennsylvania 17120, can provide information on them.

State and private lands are the heart of public hunting in Pennsylvania, however, and including the limited federal lands, they bring the total acreage available for public hunting to almost nine million.

Pennsylvania game lands provide over a million acres. There are 235 such tracts ranging in size from 91 acres in Lancaster County to 38,977 in Sullivan.

Numerous state forests and parks are also open to public hunting. They range in size from 200-acre Clearcreek State Park in Jefferson County to 266,599-acre Susquehannock State Forest in Potter County.

Cooperative programs with Pennsylvania landowners have enabled the Game Commission to open up millions of acres of private farmlands to public hunting. These vary tremendously in size. For example there are 42 farms in Wayne County that provide 3,702 acres of land for public hunting, and 406 farms in Clinton County that provide a whopping 61,000 acres of public hunting territory. Another program is the Safety Zone Program, under which 150 acres around dwellings and farm buildings are blocked off from hunting. Here, too, there is a good deal of variation as to size. Montgomery County has 3 tracts totaling 216 acres, but Venango County has 317 tracts totaling 149,521 acres.

Information on the various state hunting lands is available from the Game Commission.

Hunting on private lands other than those under some form of agreement with the Game Commission can be prohibited by fencing, posting with signs, or verbally. Landowners will often give permission to hunt, however.

There is also limited public hunting on the Indian reservation in the Allegheny National Forest, and information is available from the forest supervisor.

Pennsylvania's deer hunting rates with the best in the nation, and good public hunting lands are numerous. Potter is traditionally the best deer county in the state, however. Here the big Susquehannock State Forest offers 266,599 acres of public hunting, and the Lyman Run State Park offers another 600. Game lands also provide many acres of good deer territory. There are sizeable tracts near Emporium in Cameron County, near Philipsburg in Centre, near Farrandville in Clinton, near Johnsonburg in Elk, near English Center in Lycoming, near Betual in McKean, and near Tioga in Tioga.

This same area is the top wild-turkey country in Pennsylvania, and the game lands near Roulette, Galeton, Coudersport, Tioga, Johnsonburg, and Emporium are good. The big Susquehannock State Forest is also good for turkeys. Lycoming County often leads the state in the bear kill and game lands in the county offer good hunting—when open seasons are held. The Tiadaghton State Forest is also good.

The best pheasant hunting in the state is found in York, Lancaster, Chester, and Delaware Counties where game lands near Rossville, Franklintown, Hopeland, Bowmansville, Elstonville, and Warwick, and safety zones in Delaware County offer public hunting.

Some of the best grouse hunting occurs in Crawford and Venango Counties where there are thousands of acres of public hunting land. The Pymatuning State Park alone offers 18,575 acres of good territory, and there are 87,453 acres of safety-zone lands in Crawford and 149,521 in Venango. There are also game lands near Guys Mills, Conneaut Lake,

Hartstown, Franklin, Dempseytown, and Van, plus many others.

The best woodcock hunting is found in northeastern Sullivan County, where the Wyoming State Forest, 27,561 acres of safety zone lands, and game lands near Lopez and Sonestown offer ample public hunting opportunities. Farm Game Cooperative Program lands in Adams County are the best bet for quail.

The best, and possibly the only appreciable, snowshoe-rabbit hunting is in the northeast where game lands in Bradford, Columbia, Luzerne, Monroe, Northumberland, and Susquehanna Counties offer fair hunting. The Tioga State Forest, Lackawanna State Forest, Delaware State Forest, and Big Pocono State Park offer hunting opportunities.

Cottontail rabbits range just about all over the state, and any of the game lands, Farm Cooperative Program lands, or safety-zone lands are likely to offer good bunny-hunting.

Squirrels, too, are likely to be found anywhere that there are good tracts of hardwoods, and the state forests should all offer squirrel hunting.

The same is true of raccoons.

All of the farmlands offer woodchuck hunting.

The best waterfowl hunting is generally found in the northwest where the Pymatuning Waterfowl Area is the choice hunting area. There is good jump shooting along the Susquehanna River.

Most Pennsylvanians are avid hunters—and for a good reason.

39 • RHODE ISLAND—Small but Surprising

In a state of only 1,214 square miles and almost a million people, there would appear to be very little room for game. Surprisingly, though, there is some reasonably good hunting in the tiny New England state.

Rabbit hunters reap the richest harvest, with both cottontails and snowshoe hares present. The hare kill is small, but the hunting attracts a good deal of attention. Gray squirrels are reasonably abundant where there is suitable habitat, and the modest white-tailed deer herd is a tribute to modern game management capable of maintaining big-game hunting in such a small, densely populated state.

Raccoons, foxes, and woodchucks round out the state's game animals.

Ruffed grouse are reasonably plentiful, and there is a small, self-sustaining population of ring-necked pheasants. Quail are present on many farms, and Rhode Island is one of the few northern states offering dove shooting. There are also snipes and rails and reasonably good woodcock hunting.

The waterfowl hunting, once fabulous, still offers good shooting for those hunters willing to work for it. Brant populations are spotty, but there is reasonably good shooting for sea ducks.

A lowlands state, only eight hundred feet at its highest point, Rhode Island terrain is easy to hunt.

Public hunting land is limited and there are no national forests or other federal lands available for public hunting as is the case in so many parts of America.

On the other hand, the Rhode Island Department of Natural Resources has done a remarkable job of maintaining sizeable chunks of

Rabbit hunters reap the richest harvest in Rhode Island. *Photo by Bob Gooch.*

wildlife land in a region in which space is at a premium.

At present, there are seventeen wildlife-management areas, totaling over 30,000 acres. Arcadia State Management Area in west-central Rhode Island provides 7,523 acres of prime hunting land. Most game species found in the state are present. The smallest, 111-acre Newton Swamp State Management Area, is a good waterfowl hunting area.

All of these management areas are shown on the *Rhode Island Recreation Map*, available from the Rhode Island Department of Natural Resources, Division of Fish and Game, 83 Park Street, Providence, Rhode Island 02903.

In spite of its dense population, there is a fair amount of hunting on private lands in Rhode Island. The posting law is simple. It states that land on which the owner desires to prohibit hunting must be conspicuously posted. This is interpreted to mean the hunter must be able to see at least one posted sign from any place on the property. There are local trespass laws, however, so the best policy is to ask when in doubt.

Cottontail rabbits probably receive the heaviest hunting pressure of all game in the state. Most of the annual cottontail harvest comes from private lands, but there is reasonably good rabbit hunting on many of the management areas. Among the better ones are Arcadia, Black Hut, Buck Hill, Carolina, George Washington, and Great Swamp. These same areas support modest populations of snowshoe hares, though the hare kill is light.

The white-tailed deer is the sole big-game animal in Rhode Island. The herds are usually substantial enough to permit either-sex hunting. Good management areas include Arcadia, Black Hut, Buck Hill, Woody Hill, Burlingame, Carolina, Durfee Hill, and George Washington.

Raccoons, reasonably abundant, are found on Arcadia, Black Hut, Buck Hill, Great Swamp, and Indian Swamp.

The gray squirrel, second to the cottontail rabbit in popularity, is found on many privately owned lands, but Durfee Game Management Area is considered a top public-hunting spot. Other good ones include those described for deer and raccoons.

The ruffed grouse is probably the top game bird in Rhode Island. Much of the hunting is on private lands in the extreme northwest corner of the state, but the Buck Hill Game Management Area in this corner of the state is a fair grouse hunting area. The ruffed grouse is the top game bird on big Arcadia Game Management Area and is found on most of the others with the exception of Newton, Sapowet, and a couple of others. Grouse appear as huntable game on most of the other management areas.

The self-sustaining pheasant population supports fair hunting on private lands and on some of the management areas. Sapowet State is by far the best for pheasants, though the area is small—only 180 acres. Pheasant hunting is fair on Arcadia, Great Swamp, Indian Cedar Swamp, Durfee Hill, and a few others.

Quail hunting, spotty at best, is found on both private and public lands. Arcadia, Burlingame, Carolina, Great Swamp, Indian Cedar, Sapowet, and Woody Hill list quail.

The private potato fields in Washington County support the major dove hunting, but there are also doves on Arcadia, Black Hut, Burlingame, Carolina, Durfee Hill, Great Swamp, Indian Cedar, Sapowet, and Woody Hill Game Management Areas.

Sapowet Game Management Area supports a modest amount of hunting for both snipes and rails, and the best woodcock hunting is found in Arcadia. Woodcocks are also found on most of the areas listed for grouse, and the two birds can be hunted together. Snipes and rails are reasonably abundant on private lands and marshes along the coast.

Waterfowl hunting, not the exciting shooting it once was in Rhode Island, is still fair. Pass shooting from rock blinds along Narragansett Bay is still popular, and there is some jump shooting on inland streams and ponds. Offshore blinds suppport the bulk of the waterfowling today, however. Points of land, such as Point Judith and Sakonnet Point that jut into Block Island and Rhode Island Sounds, are good examples.

Good game-management areas include Newton Swamp, Woody Hill, Durfee Hill, Carolina, Great Swamp, and Sapowet. Puddle ducks and geese are the major species in these Areas.

The fact that densely populated Rhode Island can still support good hunting offers hope to Americans everywhere as they dejectedly watch suburbia creep into their favorite hunting grounds.

40 • SOUTH CAROLINA—Top Bobwhite Country

An abundance of bobwhite quail, doves, wild turkeys, and long, liberal deer-seasons in the famous Low Country make South Carolina a hunting paradise. Public hunting opportunities are limited, unfortunately.

Approximately half of South Carolina's hunters go after the popular bobwhite and mourning dove. In parts of the state, the dove is ahead of the quail in popularity. The annual bag for each game bird runs in excess of two million birds. Wild turkey hunting is excellent with the best on the managed game-management areas. There is also much good turkey hunting on the vast private lands. Deer hunting begins as early as mid-August in some of the coastal regions and continues through the calendar year. Bag limits are liberal—up to five deer per season.

Private lands and social clubs support the bulk of the hunting in South Carolina, but the Wildlife and Marine Resources Department is expanding its game-management areas as fast as financial resources and available land permit. These areas support the bulk of the game-management programs that have made significant strides in wild turkey restoration and in other areas of wildlife management.

Two national forests, providing over one-half million acres of public hunting land, make up the major federal lands in South Carolina.

The Sumter National Forest is broken up into three sections which collectively offer 341,624 acres of public hunting land. One section is located in the north-central region between Spartanburg and Columbia, one in the extreme northwest west of Greenville, and one on the Georgia border northwest of Augusta.

The Francis Marion National Forest, offering another 245,650 acres

Tom Rodgers, founder of the National Wild Turkey Federation, with a South Carolina gobbler. *Photo by Bob Gooch.*

of public hunting land on the coast, is located in the southeast just north of Charleston.

Good maps and general information can be obtained by writing to the forest supervisosr of the forest under consideration, Columbia, South Carolina 29201.

Lands adjacent to the Clark Hill and Hartwell U.S. Army Corps of Engineers Reservoirs on the Georgia border in the western part of the state also offer thousands of acres of public hunting. Information on Hartwell can be obtained by writing the Resource Manager, Hartwell Project, U.S. Army Corps of Engineers, P.O. Box 278, Hartwell, Georgia 30643, and information on Clark Hill from the Resource Manager, Clark Hill Project, U.S. Army Corps of Engineers, Clark Hill, South Carolina 29821.

The Wildlife and Marine Resources Department can provide information on the Atomic Energy Commission land in Aiken and Barnwell Counties, and on the Santee, Carolina Sandhills, Cape Romaine, and Savannah National Wildlife Refuges.

Possibly the very best public hunting in South Carolina, however, will be found on the 1.6 million acres of game-managaement areas under the supervision of the South Carolina Wildlife and Marine Resources Commission. Many of these lands are on national forest lands. All are plainly marked. Any lands not so marked are usually privately owned and not open to public hunting without the permission of the owner.

The major game-management-area lands are Central Piedmont Hunt Unit, the Western Piedmont Hunt Unit, the Mountain Hunt Unit, and the Francis Marion Game Management Area lands. The Central Piedmont Hunt Unit comprising 640,000 acres is the largest in the state.

An excellent booklet called *Game Management Areas of South Carolina*, describing these management areas and including maps of the individual areas, can be obtained from the South Carolina Wildlife and Marine Resources Department, P.O. Box 167, Dutch Plaza, Building D, Columbia, South Carolina 29202.

The department can also furnish information on the Manchester and Sandhills State Forests.

South Carolina, with a land area of 31,055 square miles and a population of a little over two and one-half million, is not crowded. There is good hunting on the vast private lands of the state, and it is this land that the resident hunter looks to for most of his game.

However, all lands in South Carolina are considered posted as private property unless otherwise marked by signs. The hunter needs the permission of the landowner to enter such lands. Many government, corporate, and individual landowners have made their lands available to the public for hunting, and such lands are clearly marked through the Wildlife and Marine Resources Department's game-management program.

The bobwhite quail, one of the top game birds in the state, is hunted primarily on private lands, with the heaviest populations generally in the southern part of the state. The popular bird is found statewide, however. Good game-management areas include those with cut-over timber such as found on the Central Piedmont Hunt Unit. Public drawings are held in October for quail hunts on the Webb Wildlife Center.

Dove hunting is often a social affair, with invitational hunts on the big plantations. There are also many private dove fields open to hunting for a modest fee. The Wildlife and Marine Resources Department has adopted a practice of either planting and managing fields for dove shooting, or of leasing harvested fields from private owners for this purpose. A letter to the department will bring a list of such fields. The hunter who goes to the trouble of obtaining this list can enjoy some truly great dove shooting.

Deer hunting with hounds is popular in the low country of South Carolina, and the season is long on private lands, but more restricted on the game-management areas. Francis Marion Game Management Area is among the better deer territories. This area also has an abundance of feral hogs that can be hunted during the regular deer season. Other good areas include Buist in Horry County, and the Western Piedmont Hunt Unit.

Because restoration efforts have so far been limited to game-management areas, the best turkey hunting will be found on these areas. The Western Piedmont Hunt Unit is a good choice.

The major waterfowl-hunting area is big Santee-Cooper Game Management Area in Orangeburg County. Hunters are selected by drawing. Information on the drawings is available from the department.

Rabbits and squirrels are fairly abundant all over the state. Both of the national forests and all of the game-management areas offer hunting for both rabbits and squirrels. The Mountain Hunt Unit is tops for squirrels. The best cottontail hunting, however, will probably be found on private lands.

Ruffed grouse in the extreme northwest, woodcocks, snipes, rails, and a few bears, opossums, raccoons, and foxes round out the rich variety of game found in South Carolina. Wild hogs in the Francis Marion National Forest and on some of the game-management areas add an interesting new angle to big-game hunting.

Hunting is good in South Carolina.

41 • SOUTH DAKOTA—The Pheasant Capital

Back in the 1940's, the golden years of pheasant hunting in the big plains state, someone estimated the South Dakota pheasant population at fifty million birds. Happy hunters labeled the state the Pheasant Capital of the world. Changes in land-use patterns have not been good for the gaudy ringneck, however, and the populations have bounced up and down like a rubber ball. Just recently, the Department of Game, Fish, and Parks has launched an ambitious pheasant-restoration plan.

In addition to pheasants, bird hunters can expect sharp-tailed grouse, a few ruffed grouse, prairie chickens, Hungarian partridge, snipes and bobwhite quail. Both sage grouse and mourning doves are present, but are protected.

The waterfowl hunting ranks with the best and includes ducks, geese, and sandhill cranes.

The small-game hunter will find both cottontail and jackrabbits and a few fox squirrels. There are also foxes, bobcats, coyotes, and raccoons.

While South Dakota is not noted as a big-game state, there is reasonably good antelope hunting, both mule- and white-tailed-deer hunting, good wild-turkey hunting, and fair elk hunting in the Black Hills. Antelope and elk hunting are for residents only, however.

Federal lands are not abundant in South Dakota, though the Black Hills National Forest provides a good deal of public hunting land in the western part of the state. Maps and hunting information can be obtained from the forest supervisor at Custer, South Dakota 57730. The Custer National Forest offers scattered patches of public hunting land in the northwestern part of the state. The forest supervisor is located at Custer

National Forest, P.O. Box 2556; Billings, Montana 59103.

South Dakota also has scattered patches of Bureau of Land Management holdings. Maps and hunting information can be secured from the Bureau of Land Management State Office, 316 North 26th Street, Billings, Montana 59103.

The national grasslands hold good game, and, collectively, Buffalo Gap, Fort Pierce, and Grand River Grasslands provide almost 900,000 acres of public hunting. Maps and information on these lands can be obtained by writing the Central Plains Forestry Office, Chadron, Nebraska 69337. Another source of information is Custer National Forest Headquarters at the Billings, Montana, address.

The waterfowl-production areas, administered by the U.S. Fish and Wildlife Service, also offer a good deal of public hunting for the state's fine waterfowl. A good map and information on these areas can be obtained from the U.S. Fish and Wildlife Service, Box 1897, Bismarck, North Dakota 58501. There are over one-hundred such areas in the eastern part of the state, providing hunting for other game as well as waterfowl.

Over one-tenth of South Dakota's total area is made up of Indian reservations. Most are open to public hunting. The tribal councils control hunting on the reservations, issuing licenses and opening and closing areas and seasons. The hunting varies in quality.

The South Dakota Department of Game, Fish, and Parks, has for years been slowly purchasing and adding to its own holdings for public hunting. There are now well over four hundred public shooting areas, and they offer possibly the best public hunting land in the state. Totaling only 130,000 acres, the combined area is small when compared with the various federal lands, but these lands are managed for wildlife and they are productive.

Most of the state lands are small, averaging from fifty to three hundred acres, with a few going over one thousand acres and about three over three thousand. They are well-distributed throughout the better hunting country.

An excellent little guide called *South Dakota Guide to Public Shooting Areas* is available from the Department of Game, Fish, and Parks, Pierre, South Dakota 57501. It gives information as to the size of each area, its location in relation to convenient towns, and the county in which it is located. It also gives like information on the waterfowl-production areas mentioned above.

While there is an abundance of public land in South Dakota, approximately 90 percent of the land is privately owned. Farms and ranches

South Dakota is famous for its pheasant hunting. *Photo by Bob Gooch.*

support the bulk of the hunting, particularly for resident hunters. The population is scattered widely over the state's 77,047 square miles. I have hunted private lands for days without seeing another hunter. Farmers and ranches are generally friendly, and securing permission to hunt their lands is not usually difficult.

Laws governing trespass are complicated, however. They can be simplified if the hunter will remember to hunt on foot only, to hunt during established seasons, and to ask permission to enter private lands.

Pheasants and sharp-tailed grouse are the birds that attract national attention to South Dakota and lure hunters within its borders. Together, they pretty much blanket the state, though the pheasant populations are down drastically at the present. While pheasants are found throughout much of the state, the country east of the Missouri River is the real pheasant heartland. Sharptails, on the other hand, are most abundant in the grasslands of central and western South Dakota. The hunting is best west of the Missouri River, however.

The Missouri River and the northeastern and southeastern corners of the state offer the best of what is truly great waterfowl hunting. The Missouri River Waterfowl Refuges, Lake Oahe, Lake Sharpe, Lake Francis Case, and Lake Lewis and Clark, are all good.

White-tailed deer hunting is good statewide, but the best mule-deer hunting is in the West, primarily outside of the Black Hills.

South Dakota is a bird hunter's state, however, thanks to the gaudy ring-necked pheasant now suffering a severe slump. But the popular birds will be back. In the meantime, the sharp-tailed-grouse hunting is among the best in America.

42 • TENNESSEE—Deer, Boar, and Small Game

With rugged mountains stretching six thousand feet skyward along its eastern border, Tennessee is famed for its hill country, a combination of rolling foothills and picturesque mountains. To the far west, however, along the muddy Mississippi River, the country flattens out considerably.

Four and one-half million people live in its 42,244 square miles.

The white-tailed deer is the state's most popular big-game animal. There are a few bears, but the hunting is limited. Wild-boar hunting attracts a good deal of national attention, but it, too, is extremely restricted. Under careful management, the wild-turkey flocks are increasing.

The bobwhite quail has long been a favorite of the upland bird hunters, but today the mourning dove harvest exceeds the annual quail bag. There is good ruffed-grouse hunting, but most of it is tough mountain hunting. Also present are a few woodcocks and snipes, but most are taken by hunters out for other game—often grouse or quail.

Tennessee has some excellent waterfowl hunting. Historic Reelfoot Lake, the shallow, earthquake-formed depression along the Mississippi River, is nationally known. The spread of the famous Tennessee Valley Authority impoundments has made the state more attractive to both ducks and geese.

The squirrel is the number one small-game animal in Tennessee, and both gray and fox squirrels are present. Cottontail rabbits are abundant, as are woodchucks and both red and gray foxes. There are a few bobcats. Raccoons are extremely plentiful, and night hunting is a top sport. An abundance of opossums add variety to night hunting.

180

A young Tennessee bow hunter and a fine white-tailed deer. *Courtesy of Tennessee Wildlife Resources Agency.*

The Cherokee National Forest, 600,437 acres of mountain land in the eastern part of the state, is the major federal hunting land in Tennessee. Headquarters are Cleveland, Tennessee 37311. Write there for maps and hunting information.

There are also three federal military areas in the state that collectively offer over one-hundred thousand acres of public hunting lands. They are the Arnold Engineering and Development Command, Fort Campbell Army Base on the Kentucky border, and the Volunteer Ordinance Plant. Fort Campbell, with eighty thousand acres, is the major one for public hunting. Write the Tennessee Wildlife Resources Agency, Ellington Agricultural Center, P. O. Box 40747, Nashville, Tennessee 37204, for information.

The famous Land Between the Lakes area on the Kentucky-Tennessee border is a popular hunting area and information is available from Land Between the Lakes, Golden Pond, Kentucky 42231.

The best source of information for the various Tennessee Valley Authority lands and the lands of the U. S. Army Corps of Engineers is the Tennessee Wildlife Resources Agency.

The 650,000 acres of land, either owned by the Tennessee Wildlife Resources Agency or under cooperative agreement with the agency, form the heart of public hunting in Tennessee. These wildlife-management areas are scattered throughout the state from the rugged mountains in the East to the Mississippi River floodplain. Major ones include Anderson Tully, Carter Mountain, Catoosa, Cheatham, Chuck Swan, Natchez Trace, Prentice Cooper, Reelfoot and Shelby Forest. These Areas are shown on a handy little map that can be obtained from the Wildlife Resources Agency. Many of the areas are owned by the agency, but others are on private or federal lands or the lands of other state agencies. The largest are in the Cherokee National Forest.

In addition to those timber company lands under cooperative agreements with the Wildlife Resources Agency, there are also others open to public hunting under a variety of arrangements.

Public hunting lands in Tennessee total over three million acres.

While deer can be found just about all over the state, the best hunting is in the western half. Fort Campbell Military Reservation is one of the best whitetail-hunting areas in the state, and the Arnold Engineering and Development Command is also good. Good kills are made on the wildlife-management areas along the Mississippi River. The Catoosa Wildlife Management Area is good in the eastern part of the state.

The Tellico Portion of the Cherokee Wildlife Management Area, where managed hunts are held, normally produces the best bear and wild boar hunting.

Wild turkeys are making a strong comeback with the best hunting at present on the Shelby Forest Wildlife Management Area. Other good Wildlife Management Areas include Catoosa, Central Peninsula, and Nachez. The Land Between the Lakes is also good.

While the quail hunting is best on private lands, the Percy Priest Wildlife Management Area and the Arnold Engineering and Development Command, known as the AEDC Wildlife Management Area, offer good hunting. Catoosa Wildlife Management Area is also good.

These same areas offer good dove-shooting. Other good dove possibilities include Blythe Ferry and Cheatham Wildlife Management Areas and the Camden Waterfowl Area. The Cherokee National Forest offers thousands of acres of grouse hunting. Good wildlife-management areas include Catoosa, Central Peninsula, and Chickasaw.

Between the Mississippi River, the huge impoundments, Reelfoot Lake, and many winding streams where jump shooting is popular, Tennessee offers the waterfowler almost unlimited opportunities. The Mississippi River is a long-established migration route. Reelfoot Lake, which includes the Reelfoot Lake Refuge in the northwestern tip of the state, is famous for its duck hunting, particularly for mallards. Many professional guides work this area. Kentucky and Chickamauga Lakes are among the best impoundments for the duck and goose hunter. Good wildlife-management areas include Barkley, Cheatham Reservoir, and Gooch. The Land Between the Lakes Area also offers good waterfowl hunting.

With both gray and fox squirrels present, the squirrel is the number one small-game animal in Tennessee, and found just about all over the state where good stands of hardwoods exist. The Cherokee National Forests is excellent. Good wildlife-management areas include Anderson-Tully, Prentice Cooper, and Shelby Forest. The Land Between the Lakes Area is excellent. Anderson-Tully is also good for rabbits, as are Chickasaw and Laurel Hill Wildlife Management Areas.

Just about all of the public hunting lands offer raccoon and opossum for the night hunters.

Tennessee hunters enjoy a wide variety of good hunting.

43 • TEXAS—Big and Varied

Limited public hunting, but excellent hunting for a wide variety of game, is a brief summation of hunting in Texas. Twelve million people live in Texas's widespread 265,842 square miles.

Both mule and white-tailed deer, antelope, Aoudad sheep, pumas, javelinas, and wild turkeys provide the big-game hunter with a good selection of game. Desert bighorns, now protected, offer hope for hunting in the future.

Quail—bobwhite and blue, plus a few Gambel's and Mearn's—are the top game birds in Texas, and in good seasons they are extremely abundant. Possibly of equal importance to the bird hunter is the state's fine dove shooting. Texas is one of the best dove states. Mourning doves provide the bulk of the hunting, but there is also reasonably good white-winged dove shooting near the Mexican border. Texas is not a good ring-necked pheasant state, though there is limited hunting. There is also an open season on the chachalaca, by rights a Mexican bird that has ignored international boundaries. There is also limited prairie-chicken hunting, some woodcock hunting, good snipe hunting, and fair rail hunting.

The small-game hunter finds Texas generous with its cottontail rabbits and jackrabbits, both of which are abundant, and also fine hunting for both gray and fox squirrels.

For the varmint hunter, there are both gray and red foxes, armadillos, coyotes, prairie dogs, ground squirrels, Russian boars, bobcats, raccoons, and opossums—all unprotected.

Waterfowl hunting is good along the coast and in some inland areas. Ducks, geese, and sandhill cranes make up the waterfowl populations in Texas.

Public hunting land in Texas is extremely limited. By far the best hunting is found on the vast private lands, mostly the big ranches.

Federal hunting lands in Texas are limited to four national forests and national grasslands. The national forests are Sabine with 183,842 acres, Davy Crockett with 161,556 acres, Sam Houston with 158,204 acres, and Angelina with 154,392 acres. Headquarters for these National Forests is Lufkin, Texas 75901. Write the forest supervisor there for maps and hunting information. The national grasslands, in scattered blocks in the North and in the Texas Panhandle, provide another 117,269 acres of prairie hunting. These are Caddo National Grasslands near the Oklahoma border, Cross Timbers, Black Kettle, and Rita Blanca. For maps and hunting information, write the Regional Supervisor, U.S. Forest Service, 517 Gold Avenue, S.W., Albuquerque, New Mexico 87101.

There is some public hunting at 199,000-acre Fort Hood, but it is generally limited to Fort Hood Rod and Gun Club members. Fort Bliss offers 49,920 acres of bird and small-game hunting. Write the Commanding Officer, Fort Hood, Texas 76544, or the Commanding Officer, Fort Bliss, Texas 79906, for hunting details.

Ten wildlife-management areas managed by the Texas Parks and Wildlife Commission, 4200 Smith School Road, Austin, Texas 78701, offer limited hunting, but they are not always open. They are held primarily for game-research work. Among them, however, are Angelina, Black Gap, Gene Howe, Gus Engling, J. D. Murphree, Kerr, Matador, and Sierra Diablo. Write the commission for hunting details.

Since private lands support the bulk of hunting in Texas, these lands become of utmost importance to the hunter. The posting law in Texas is simple. It says it is illegal to hunt on privately owned lands without the consent of the owner or the owner's agent. The hunting rights to much of the private land in Texas are leased to individuals or clubs, but there is usually land that the average person can hunt if he will take the trouble to courteously approach the owner. Many ranches offer hunting by the day on a fee basis.

White-tailed deer are found statewide with the south-central region and the southern brush country particularly good. The Edwards Plateau is a good whitetail area. Mule deer are most abundant in the western portion of the state, close to the New Mexico border.

The antelope hunting does not compare with that of the better-known antelope states, but there is fair hunting in the western part of the state, noteably the Trans-Pecos, the Panhandle, and the Permian Basin.

Javelinas are found throughout the southern one-third of the big state,

Outdoor writer. Robert Elman and a fine Texas white-tailed deer. *Courtesy of Popular Guns magazine.*

and are plentiful in the Big Bend Country and in the brush country of the South.

Aoudad are designated as game animals in eight northwestern counties, but occur on several private ranches throughout the state. Hunting is regulated in the eight counties at present, but elsewhere there is no closed season or bag limit.

The Rio Grande turkey is found primarily in the western two-thirds of the state, in the land of wooded hills covered with live and Spanish oak and Texas cedar.

The best bobwhite-quail hunting is in the eastern two-thirds of the state, while the blue or scaled quail is most abundant in the western two-thirds of Texas. It is abundant in the Big Bend Country. The best mourning-dove hunting is in South Texas, but the birds are found just about all over Texas. The best white-winged dove shooting is along the Mexican border and in South Texas generally.

There are a few pheasants and prairie chickens in the Panhandle near the Oklahoma border, and chachalaca are found in the extreme southeastern part of the state.

The best woodcock hunting is along the Louisiana border, and there is good snipe hunting along the coastal marshes and in the prairie rice fields. Large king rails are plentiful in the rice country of east Texas.

The gray squirrel is abundant in east Texas where it is a highly regarded game animal. Fox squirrels are also found in the East, but in different habitat. Its range extends much further west, however, to the pecan bottoms of the central part of the state.

Cottontails are extremely abundant in the northern and eastern parts of Texas, and in the southern brush country. Jackrabbits are abundant throughout the western part of the state. Foxes are found mostly in the east, and coyotes are abundant in West Texas and in the Panhandle. Bobcats, found statewide, are abundant in the southern and western parts of the state. Raccoons and opossums are reasonably abundant just about all over Texas.

The best waterfowl hunting is along the coast in the rice country and the wet prairies. Snow, Canada, and white-fronted geese, and a wide variety of ducks frequent this country. Professional guides work this area, and this is possibly the best bet for the hunter. Ducks also flock to the watering tanks across South Texas.

While it offers rich and varied hunting, Texas is one of the most complicated states to hunt.

44 • UTAH—Mule Deer, Elk, and Cougars

A good variety of big game, an even wider variety of game birds, and excellent waterfowl hunting make Utah a fine hunting state. Its highest mountain peak stretches to 13,528 feet, but there are many square miles of desert and big, semiarid country. Over a million people live in its eighty-five thousand square miles of rugged, but scenic, country.

The big-game hunter will find excellent mule-deer hunting, some of the best cougar hunting in America, black-bear hunting, good elk-hunting, and antelope, moose, bighorn-sheep, and buffalo hunting for residents only. There are also spring and fall hunting for wild turkeys.

The bird hunter can have a ball in Utah, but the wide variety of game will frustrate him as he attempts to settle on a single species. The ring-necked pheasant is the most popular game bird, but mourning doves are a strong second. The chukar-partridge hunting is almost as good as the dove and pheasant hunting, and the Hungarian-partridge hunting is reasonably good, but spotty. Blue, ruffed, and sage grouse offer fair hunting for the grouse enthusiasts. There is good quail-hunting in the state. The Gambel's is native to Utah, and both the California and mountain quail have been introduced.

With an estimated 400,000 acres of marshlands, Utah offers excellent hunting for both ducks and geese. Hunting for whistling swans was permitted for the first time in 1963, and annual seasons have been held since. Normally, twenty-five hundred permits are issued.

The small-game list in Utah is not impressive, but there is fair hunting for cottontail rabbits. Both black-tailed and white-tailed jackrabbits are abundant and unprotected. There are also snowshoe hares in the mountains. They are protected, but there is usually a winter season. Abert squirrels are fully protected, but there are no closed seasons on other species of squirrels. Coyotes and foxes are plentiful, but both bobcats and crows are protected.

Public lands in Utah are plentiful—7.2 percent state-owned, 67.1 percent in federal ownership, 4.2 percent in Indian reservations, and only 21.5 percent privately owned. Hunting opportunities are almost unlimited.

National forests provide 8.25 million acres of hunting land in Utah. Most are wholly within the state. The Ashley National Forest is headquartered at Vernal, UT 84078; Cache National Forest at Logan, UT 84321; Dixie National Forest at Cedar City, UT 84720; Fishlake National Forest at Richfield, UT 84701; Manti-LaSal National Forest at Price, UT 84501; Uinta National Forest at Provo, UT 84601; the Wasatch National Forest at Salt Lake City, UT 84101; the Sawtooth National Forest at Twin Falls, 83301; and Caribou National Forest, headquartered at Pocatello, ID 83201. Write the forest supervisor at the headquarters of the forest you are interested in. Ask for maps and hunting information, and for a handy little booklet called *A Guide to National Forest Recreation in Utah.*

In addition to the national forest lands, the Bureau of Land Management lands offer many acres of additional public hunting in Utah. Maps and information on these lands can be obtained from the U.S. Department of Interior, Washington, DC 20240, or University Club Building, Salt Lake City, Utah 84111.

Lands owned by the state of Utah include several excellent waterfowl-management areas. Information on the state hunting lands can be obtained by writing the Utah Division of Wildlife, 1596 West North Temple, Salt Lake City, Utah 84116.

The Ute-Ouray, Piute, Navajo, and Goshute Indian tribes allow hunting on their lands, normally by the sale of hunting permits. Information is available from the Ute-Ouray Indian Reservation, Uinta and Ouray Agency, Fort Duchesne, UT 84026; the Piute and Goshute Indian Reservations, Branch of Land Operations, Owyhee, NV 89832; and the Navajo Indian Reservation, Branch of Land Operations, Navajo Area Office, Window Rock, AZ 86515.

Posted land in Utah is land on which posters or painted wording have been posted at approximately one-quarter-mile intervals along the exterior boundaries, at all corners, and along all roads, trails, or other rights-of-way entering such lands. It is illegal to hunt such land without the permission of the owner.

Utah is one of the top western waterfowl states. *Photo by Utah Division of Wildlife Resource.*

The best mule-deer hunting is found in the central and southern regions of the state. The Dixie and Manti-LaSal National Forests are good. Southern and eastern Utah offer the best cougar hunting. Elk are found in huntable populations in the Uinta National Forest, and this big national forest also offers the best moose hunting. The antelope hunting is best in Dagett County and on the western deserts. San Juan County is the site of the limited bighorn-sheep hunting.

The agricultural counties of Box Elder and Cache in the northwest are usually the top pheasant producers. Davis, Emery, and Weber Counties are also good. Most of the best hunting for pheasants is on private land, so the permission of the landowner is needed. The dove-hunting areas are much the same as those already mentioned for pheasants, as they too thrive best in agricultural areas. Beaver, Box Elder, Iron, Juab, and Washington Counties are among the best. Chukars are found just about statewide with the Bureau of Land Management areas offering good hunting. Box Elder, Carbon, and Uintah Counties are good. Hungarian partridge are found primarily in Box Elder, Cache, and Rich Counties along the northern border. The best sage-grouse hunting will be found in the Diamond Mountain area of Uintah County, Parker Mountain in Wayne County, and John's Valley in Garfield County. The best blue-grouse range is in the northern Wasatch Range of the Rocky Mountains, and the best ruffed-grouse hunting is in Cache National Forest.

Washington County in southern Utah is the top Gambel's quail county, and normally, Box Elder, Carbon, and Davis are among the top counties for California quail.

The Bear River Migratory Bird Refuge is one of the top waterfowl areas in Utah, but Fish Springs and Ouray also offer good hunting. These are Federal refuges, and hunting is permitted in specific areas. The state-owned, wildlife-management areas offer more hunting opportunities, however. Among the best are Farmington Bay, Harold Crane, and Ogden Bay. Clear Lake and Powell Slough are reasonably good.

Cottontail rabbits roam the state, but are particularly abundant in the southeastern county of San Juan, and in Duchesne and Uintah Counties in the North. Jackrabbits are found in the desert and foothills country, as are coyotes, bobcats, and foxes.

An ambitious hunter can keep busy all year in Utah.

45 • VERMONT—For Bears and Grouse

With almost half a million people crowded into only 9,069 square miles, it would be easy to assume that there is no hunting in this small New England state. But such an assumption would be wrong.

Vermont has one of the best white-tailed deer kills in the country when you consider that bucks only are legal for firearms hunters. Bow hunters may take antlerless animals. Both seasons are brief—only 16 days. The black-bear hunting is as good as any in the East, and there is excellent grouse and woodcock hunting. The waterfowl hunting is also good, and is well-distributed throughout the small, mountainous state.

Vermont is a ruggedly scenic state, with picturesque mountains, green valleys, clean, fast rivers, and sparkling lakes. An estimated 75 percent of the state is in forests, with evergreens predominant in the North. Private landowners control about 75 percent of the forested lands. But there is a good deal of corporate land and publicly owned land. All support hunting.

The Green Mountain National Forest, 235,000 acres of fine public hunting land, supports much of the hunting in Vermont. Headquarters for the forest are located at Rutland, Vermont 05701, where maps and general information are available. This national forest and the Missisquoi National Wildlife Refuge are the major federal lands in Vermont. Headquarters for the refuge are at Swanton, Vermont 05488.

State forests, state parks, and wildlife-management areas comprise the state-owned lands in Vermont. Hunting is generally permitted on all of these lands, even in most of the state parks. Information on hunting possibilities and regulations can be obtained from the Vermont Fish and

Game Department, Montpelier, Vermont 95602.

Key state forests include Camels Hump, Roxbury, Groton, Willoughby, Williams River, and Arlington. A dozen state parks, including Coolidge, Bomoseen, Emerald Lake, Underhill, Elmore, Brighton, and Kettle Pond, are worth checking out—particularly for forest hunting. Good wildlife-management areas include Steam Mill Brook, Hurricane Brook, Lewis Creek, Podunk, Victory Basin, and Les Newell. The wildlife-manageament areas vary in size from those like Weathersfield, with less than one hundred acres, to Hurricane Brook, with over nine thousand acres of public hunting land.

Commercial forests claim over three million acres of Vermont land, and most of this prime land is available for public hunting. Leading landowners are the St. Regis Paper Company, West Stewartstown, NH 03597; International Paper Company, Glen Falls, NY 12801; Brown Paper Company, Berlin, NH 03570; New England Electric Company, Concord NH 03301; Glastonbury Timber Lands, Bennington, VT 05201; Atlas Plywood, Morrisville, VT 05661; Ward Lumber Company, Waterbury, VT 05676; Bardill Land and Lumber Company, Wolcott, VT 05680; A. Johnson Company, Bristol, VT 05443; Groveton Paper Company, Groveton, NH 03582; and Franconia Paper Company, Lincoln, NH 03251.

Many small landowners and farmers readily give permission to hunt when approached courteously. A landowner, desiring to prohibit hunting on his property, must post the land at each corner and at intervals not in excess of four hundred feet. He must also record his posting annually with the clerk of the town in which the land is located.

Bear and deer are the big-game animals in Vermont, and both provide good hunting. The white-tailed deer is the most abundant and is found in all counties from border to border. In general, deer are the most abundant in the south and central regions, but the true trophy bucks are more likely to roam the northern region of the state. In recent seasons, the southern towns of Chester, Dorset, Pawlet, Rupert, and the central towns of Hartland, Woodstock, Norwich, Sharon, Thetford, Danville, Barent, Ryegate, Newbury, Berlin and Northfield have produced the largest deer kills.

Good bear-kills also occur pretty much statewide, but generally in the more mountainous areas. Good towns include Stratton in the south, Rochester, Granville, Orange, Warren, and Stockbridge in the central part of Vermont, and Eden, Montgomery, and Guildhall in the north.

The ruffed grouse is the most abundant upland game bird, and it, too, is found throughout the state. The Green Mountain National Forest is

Ruffed-grouse hunting is tops in Vermont. *Photo by Bob Gooch.*

good, and so are all of the state forests. Many of the state parks and wildlife-management areas are productive.

The woodcock pushes the grouse as a popular game-bird. The best hunting is generally found in the central and southern third of the state.

Wild turkeys are present in limited numbers, and open seasons are an annual affair.

Snipes and rails occur in good concentrations in the lowlands.

Mallards, black ducks, wood ducks, and blue-winged teal are Vermont's most abundant puddle ducks. Goldeneyes, scaup, mergansers, and ring-necked ducks make up the bulk of the diving-duck populatioins. The puddle ducks are found throughout the state, but migrating birds tend to follow the Champlain Valley and Connecticut Rivers. All of these puddle ducks nest in the state, however. Lake Champlain and Lake Memphremagog support most of the diving ducks. State-owned, waterfowl-management areas now total over nine thousand acres, and the Fish and Game Department is adding additional acres as they become available. Wildlife-management areas that are managed for waterfowl include Maquam Bay, East Creek, Mud Creek, and Richville Reservoir. Dead Creek Waterfowl Area supports a small flock of Canada geese.

Gray squirrels, snowshoe hares, and cottontail rabbits provide plenty of hunting for the small-game enthusiast. All public hunting lands having a reasonable amount of hardwoods to provide nuts and dens support good squirrel populations. Squirrels are most abundant in the Champlain Valley and in the southern part of the state.

Snowshoe hares occur all over the state. Swamps of cedar, fir, or spruce are good. Cottontails, like the squirrels, are most abundant in the Champlain Valley and in the southern counties.

Red fox, raccoons, woodchucks, and bobcats round out the rich variety of game birds and animals found in Vermont.

46 • VIRGINIA—Land of Varied Hunting

Quail and doves for the bird hunter, squirrels for the small-game hunter, and deer and turkeys for the big-game enthusiast, probably best describe the hunting picture in the Old Dominion.

Quail hunting is traditionally popular in the state, but in recent years, the mourning dove has pressed the bobwhite for the number one game bird. Except for a brief dove season in December, the seasons do not overlap, however, and many hunters go after both. The ruffed-grouse hunting is fair in the rugged western mountains, but the hunting is tough. Pheasant hunting is extremely limited, with various strains of birds being introduced on an experimental basis. Clapper and sora rails in the eastern marshes, woodcocks, and snipes round out the game-bird offering.

Cottontail rabbits are abundant in many parts of the state, and there are a few snowshoe hares in Highland County, but the squirrel is the number one small-game animal in the state. Gray squirrels are abundant, and there is a fair population of fox squirrels in the western mountains.

Waterfowl hunting is reasonably good, but not particularly popular among a majority of the state's hunters. Much of the better hunting is tied up in private clubs and is concentrated along the coastal marshes.

A mushrooming white-tailed deer herd, estimated at approximately 300,000 animals, furnishes an annual bag of 60,000 to 65,000 whitetails, making Virginia one of the top eastern deer-states. The wild turkey is also making a strong comeback in the state, and hunters take 5,000 to 6,000 birds annually between the fall and spring seasons. The black bear rounds out the big game picture, but bruin is running into trouble in

Virginia. An estimated population of 1,000 animals gives up a kill of approximately 150 bears annually.

Both foxes and raccoons are reasonably abundant, and there are a few bobcats in isolated areas. Woodchuck hunting is popular, and the opportunities are almost unlimited.

The George Washington and Jefferson National Forests provide one and one-half million acres of public hunting land in the western part of the state, and this land receives a good deal of attention from both resident and nonresident hunters. Maps and hunting information on George Washington are available from the Forest Supervisor, George Washington National Forest, Federal Building, Harrisonburg, Virginia 22801. The same information on Jefferson can be obtained from the Forest Supervisor, Jefferson National Forest, 3517 Brandon Avenue SW, Roanoke, Virginia 24018.

Big military bases in the East provide almost 200,000 acres of prime hunting land. The major ones are the U. S. Marine Corps Base, Quantico, VA 22134; Fort Pickett Military Reservation, Blackstone, VA 23824; and Fort A. P. Hill Military Reservation, Bowling Green, VA 22427. Hunting maps and instructions for the military lands can be obtained by writing to the commanding officer of the respective reservations.

The Chincoteague, Great Dismal Swamp, and Presquile Island National Wildlife Refuges offer limited public hunting, but regulatioins vary from year to year. Chincoteague has a rare herd of sika deer, Great Dismal Swamp has white-tailed deer, and Presquile offers good deer-hunting occasionally.

In addition to the vast and varied federal lands, The Virginia Commission of Game and Inland Fisheries, Box 11104, Richmond, Virginia 23230, owns in excess of 170,000 acres of wildlife-management-area lands. Collectively, they provide hunting for all species of game from waterfowl to bear and deer. A book called *Wildlife Management Areas* is available from the commission's Richmond office.

The Commission of Game and Inland Fisheries is responsible for the wildlife management on another 250,000 acres of land owned by other government agencies. Included are the Piedmont State Forests, several experimental forests, land of the U.S. Corps of Engineers, and several state parks where limited hunting is permitted. Information on these lands is also available from the commission office.

Private corporations are good to Virginia hunters. Together they provide another 700,000 acres of hunting on lands managed for timber. Included are the Chesapeake Corporation of Virginia, West Point, VA

The mourning dove is the number one game bird in Virginia. *Photo by Bob Gooch* .

23181; Continental Forest Industries, P.O. Box 1041, Hopewell,VA 23860; Union Camp Corporation, Franklin, VA 23851; Hoerner Waldorf Corporation, P.O. Box 580, Roanoke Rapids, NC 27870; Glatfelter Pulp Wood Company, P. O. Box 868, Fredericksburg, VA 22401; Weyerhauser Company, Plymouth, NC 27962; Appalachina Power Company, P.O. Box 2021, Roanoke, VA 24009; Lester Properties, Martinsville, VA 24112; Owens-Illinois Company, Big Island, VA 24526; Burrus Land and Lumber Company, P. O. Box 129, Lynchburg, VA 24505; and Westvaco, Route 3, Box 135A, Lynchburg, VA 24504.

Some of these companies charge a modest fee for hunting permits, while others do not. Complete information can be obtained by writing the companies.

An excellent and complete booklet called *Virginia Hunters Guide* is available for the asking from the commission office given above. It can prove invaluable for a hunter planning a trip to Virginia.

A great many private landowners readily grant hunting privileges to those who approach them courteously and show the proper respect for their rights. The Virginia posting law is one of the toughest in the nation, however. Verbal permission from the landowner is required for hunting unposted land, but written permission is needed if the land is posted.

Big-game hunters will find the best deer hunting in the George Washington National Forest in the West, but on private lands in the East. The three big military areas also offer good deer hunting. Turkey hunting is also good in the George Washington National Forest and the easternmost sections of the Jefferson National Forest. Fort A. P. Hill and Quantico Marine Corps Base also offer good turkey hunting.

The quail hunting is best in the southeastern quarter of the state and generally on private lands, though several of the wildlife-management areas offer fair quail hunting. The same is generally true of dove hunting.

Grouse hunting is best on the two national forests.

The Back Bay Hunting Areas of the Commission of Game and Inland Fisheries offer the best public hunting for waterfowl. At times, the hunting is excellent in the state.

History lures most visitors to Virginia, but the hunting is also worth a trip.

47 • WASHINGTON—For Big Game and Game Birds

With three million people and a land area of 69,000 square miles, Washington is the smallest of the contiguous western states, but it supports the largest human population outside of California. A coastal state, its rugged and varied terrain ranges from sea level to 14,408-foot Mount Rainier.

Washington hunters enjoy a wide variety of game, and seasons that open as early as September for some species and end as late as March 31 for others. Big-game animals include black bears, three subspecies of deer, elk, bighorn sheep, mountain goats, mountain lions, and wild turkeys.

The small-game hunter must choose among raccoons, rockchucks, bobcats, cottontails, snowshoes, jackrabbits, and western gray squirrels.

The bird hunter has a rich variety—pheasants, band-tailed pigeons, doves, quail, Hungarian and chukar partridge, blue, ruffed, spruce, sharp-tailed, and sage grouse, and snipes.

A wide variety of ducks, geese, and black brant make up the waterfowl populations.

Moose and caribou are protected, but there is varmint hunting for coyotes, crows, magpies, and foxes.

Public lands are abundant in Washington, with the total acreage in the neighborhood of twelve million. Large corporations that make their lands available for hunting swell the total by another 4.5 million.

The federal government is the major public landowner in Washington with eleven million acres, mostly in nine national forests. Colville National Forest contains a million acres; Kanisku, three hundred thousand; Okanogan, two million acres; Mount Baker, one and three quarters of a million acres; Olympic, seven hundred thousand acres; Wenatchee, two million acres; Snoqualmie, one and one-half million acres; Gifford Pinchot, one and one-half million acres; and Umatilla National Forest, three hundred thousand acres. Maps and hunting information on these vast forest lands can be obtained by writing the U. S. Forest Service, Pacific Northwest Region, Box 3623, Portland, Oregon 97208.

The Washington Department of Game owns and manages another 120,000 acres of prime hunting land, and information on these lands can be obtained from the Washington Department of Game, 600 North Capitol Way, Olympia, Washington 98504. The state-owned, public hunting areas range in size from a few acres to almost 100,000 acres. Many are held primarily for waterfowl management.

Among the corporations offering private lands for public hunting are Crown Zellerbach, Longview Fiber, Northern Pacific Railway, and Weyerhauser. Information on hunting these and other corporate lands can be obtained from the Department of Game or from the American Forest Products Industries, Inc., 1835 K Street NW, Washington, DC 20006.

With so much public and corporate land open for public hunting, there is little need to hunt the private lands of farmers, ranchers, and others. The hunter who does should obtain the permission of the owner before entering such lands.

The Washington black-bear hunting could well be the best in the nation. The best hunting in the entire state is found in the Olympic Peninsula region, with the northeast corner of the state and the Lower Columbia River areas also good. There are both fall and spring seasons, and the animals are actually found just about all over the state, reaching nuisance numbers in some areas.

Deer hunting falls into three categories—blacktails west of the Cascade Mountains, mule deer east of the Cascades, and whitetails in the northeast. Good counties include Clark, Cowlitz, Kitsap, Klickitat, Lewis, Mason, Okanogan, Pacific, Pierce, Stevens, Thurston, and Wahkaikum.

Roosevelt elk are found primarily on the Olympic Peninsula, the Willapa Hills in the vicinity of Mt. St. Helens, and along the western slopes of the Cascades. The Rocky Mountain elk is found in the eastern part of the state in the Yakima River Drainage, the Wenatchee Mountains, and in the Blue Mountains. Big-game hunters take well over ten thousand elk annually.

A wide variety of ducks, geese, and black brant make up the Washington waterfowl populations. *Photo by Bob Gooch.*

Mountain goats are found primarily in the Cascade Mountains where there is a good population. The animals have been introduced to the Olympic Mountains, but the best hunting will be found in the Cascades.

Bighorn sheep, once near extinct, are now available for resident hunters only. They find fair hunting in Okanogan, Columbia, Garfield, Chelan, and Kittitas counties.

The bird hunter may have more of a problem deciding what to hunt than he will finding a place to hunt.

The grouse hunter can choose between blue, ruffed, spruce, sharp-tailed, and sage grouse. The blue grouse is found in the coniferous forests along both slopes of the Cascades, while the ruffed grouse, also a bird of the forests, is found in lowland timber just about statewide. The spruce grouse inhabits the lodgepole-pine, fir, and spruce regions of the Cascades, Olympics, and the mountainous areas of northwestern Washington. The sharptail is found primarily in the grassland regions of Douglas, Lincoln, and Okanogan Counties, while the sage grouse is found also in Douglas and Lincoln Counties and in the counties of Grant, Kittitas, and Yakima.

Mourning doves are found statewide, but are especially plentiful in the Okanogan and Yakima Valleys. The band-tailed pigeon is found primarily in the western part of the state. It prefers coniferous and hard-wood forests.

Valley quail live in the agricultural valleys along both sides of the Cascades, the mountain quail in the counties of Kitsap, Thurston, and Pierce, and the scaled quail in eastern Washington in the Hanford area and the potholes country of Grant County. There are a few bobwhite quail in the lower Yakima Valley and in southeastern Washington. Gambel's quail have been introduced but have not yet reached huntable populations.

The pheasant is the most popular game-bird in Washington, however, and the Columbia Basin accounts for almost half of the annual harvest. Yakima Valley is also good.

Large populations of Hungarian partridge live in the grassy borders of the wheat fields of eastern Washington, and the chukar partridge is found primarily along the river breaks of Columbia, Okanogan, Snake, Yakima, Palouse, and Grande Pond Rivers.

Rabbits are found just about statewide, with the snowshoe hare limited to the high country.

The Columbia Basin takes first place for waterfowling, but Puget Sound and the Olympic Basin areas are also good.

There is much good hunting in Washington.

48 • WEST VIRGINIA—The Mountain State

Its beautiful mountains ravaged by both strip and deep mines, and its rich forests exploited by zealous loggers, picturesque West Virginia still offers a lot to the hunter. Roughly two million people live in its 24,181 square miles. Public lands total over a million acres, and accessible private lands add many more acres of good hunting territory.

Black bear, white-tailed deer, and wild turkeys are the big-game hunter's menu in West Virginia. The black bear, once abundant in West Virginia, has experienced threats from a mushrooming human population, just as it has throughout its vast Appalachian range, but still furnishes reasonably good hunting. The same is true of deer and turkeys. But good management has brought both back from near extinction, and the hunter will find reasonably good deer and turkey hunting.

The ruffed grouse is the number one game bird in West Virginia, leading all other species by a good margin. The annual harvest often exceeds 100,000 birds, but the hunting is tough in the rugged mountain forests. Native hunters call them "mountain pheasant." The bobwhite-quail hunting is fair in limited areas of the state. Woodcocks nest in the state and offer reasonably good hunting. They are possibly underharvested. The mourning dove is limited to certain areas, and there are a few snipes and rails. Finally, there are limited populations of pheasants in the Ohio River Valley.

With an annual bag of well over a million animals, the squirrel is easily the number one game animal in West Virginia. The little gray is by far the most abundant, but there are also a few fox squirrels, mostly along the Ohio River. The cottontail rabbit follows the squirrel in

Walking up rails in West Virginia. *Courtesy of West Virginia Department of Natural Resources.*

popularity, and there are a few snowshoes in the high mountain country. Raccoon hunting is extremely popular. Foxes and bobcats round out the small-game hunting possibilities.

West Virginia's rugged terrain does not lend itself to duck hunting, but there is limited waterfowling. The best is found along the Ohio and Potomac Rivers, but there is some jump shooting along the New River and other streams throughout the state.

Big Monongahela National Forest, sprawling over the mountainous eastern part of the state, offers 808,898 acres of federal land. It is the major public-hunting area in the state. An additional 110,000 acres of the George Washington National Forest spill over from Virginia. for information and maps of the Monongahela National Forest, write the Forest Supervisor, Monongahela National Forest, Elkins, West Virginia 26241. Headquarters for the George Washington National Forest is The Federal Building, Harrisonburg, Virginia 22801.

Lands adjacent to the U. S. Army Corps of Engineers' Bluestone and Tygart Reservoirs provide another 20,000 acres of public hunting land.

Information on hunting these lands can be obtained from the West Virginia Department of Natural Resources, 1800 Washington Street East, Charleston, West Virginia 25303.

In addition to the vast federal lands, the Department of Natural Resources owns or leases another 161,000 acres of West Virginia land, and hunting is permitted on the state forests, totaling 77,000 acres. The public hunting areas range in size from 778-acre Williams River Public Hunting Area to 21,114-acre Sleepy Creek Public Hunting Area. State forests range in size from 5,578-Camp Creek to 13,251-acre Coopers Rock.

In the land where the Hatfields and McCoys lived by the gun, resident landowners are permitted to carry uncased guns at any time in caring for their livestock. However, it is illegal to shoot, hunt, or trap upon the fenced, enclosed, or posted lands of another without first obtaining permission from the owner. Posted signs must be legally printed, easily discernible, and conspicuously placed. There is, however, a good deal of private land available for hunting, some of it for a fee. Several large timber corporations permit hunting under varying arrangements. Details on these lands can be obtained by writing the Department of Natural Resources.

The Monongahela National Forest is a good choice for deer hunting. The counties of Greenbrier, Pocahontas, Randolph, and Tucker all offer good deer hunting, and portions of these counties lie in the national forest. Good public hunting areas include Chief Cornstalk, Elk River, Lewis Wetzel, Sleepy Creek, and Williams River. The Kumbrabow, Seneca, Calvin Price, and Coopers Rock State Forests are also worth investigating.

The Monongahela National Forest is also the best bet for the bear hunter. Good counties include Greenbrier, Pocahontas, Randolph, and Tucker.

Turkeys, too, are abundant on the National Forest lands, and the Eastern Panhandle counties are generally good. Some of the best hunting is on private lands. Bluestone, Fork Creek, Chief Cornstalk, Short Mountain, Williams River, and Sleepy Creek Public Hunting Areas also hold turkey populations. So do the Kumbrabow, Seneca, Calvin Price, and Coopers Rock State Forests.

Grouse are found in just about every county in West Virginia, so finding huntable populations of the popular birds is seldom a problem. Much of the good hunting occurs in farm woodlots and on private lands, but the two national forests offer the best hunting opportunities. Good public hunting areas include Bluestone, Elk River, Fork Creek, Lewis

Wetzel, Nathaniel Mountain, Short Mountain, Williams River, and Sleepy Creek. The state forests are all likely to hold fair grouse populations. The better ones are Kumbrabow, Seneca, Coopers Rock, and Kanawha.

Squirrels, too, are abundant statewide. Again, the national forests, with their vast stands of timber, are good choices. The big timber companies all own good squirrel woods, particularly along the creeks and branches. Most of the fox squirrels, however, are found along the Ohio River and in the eastern counties of Greenbrier, Hardy, and Hampshire. All of the state forests hold good gray squirrel populations, and most of the public hunting areas do also.

Pheasants are generally limited to the Ohio River Valley and the northern Panhandle counties. The Lewis Wetzel Public Hunting Area is a good bet for rabbits, though the best hunting is on farmlands. The famous Canaan Valley is tops for woodcocks, and one of the best timberdoodle-hunting areas in the East, but there is little or no public hunting land.

Quail hunting is best along the river valleys and on the eastern farms.

West Virginians are outdoor-loving people, and hunting rates high with them. Fortunately, they enjoy many opportunities.

49 • WISCONSIN—For Hunting Opportunities

With the state alone owning approximately 6.5 million acres of land, most of which is open for public hunting, Wisconsin is truly a land of hunting opportunities.

White-tailed deer and black bears comprise the big-game family, and hunting for both is good.

There are cottontail rabbits, jackrabbits, and snowshoe hares, plus squirrels, bobcats, foxes, and raccoons for the small-game enthusiast. The bird hunter will find excellent ruffed-grouse and woodcock hunting, fair-to-good hunting for pheasants, Hungarian partridge, and some hunting for sharp-tailed grouse, bobwhite quail, snipes, and rails.

Blessed with an abundance of water, Wisconsin hunters enjoy good waterfowling throughout the state.

The wild turkey populations are struggling, and it is not likely that these magnificent birds will ever prosper in this cold northern state.

Mourning doves, spruce grouse, prairie chickens, moose, elk, timber wolves, badgers, and lynx are fully protected.

Wisconsin has an area of 56,154 square miles which comfortably supports 4.5 million people.

Federal lands in Wisconsin are confined generally to two large national forests, the Chequamegon with 831,000 acres and the Nicolet with 643,875 acres. The Chequamegon, separated into three blocks, is located in the northwest and north-central part of the state. Maps and hunting information may be obtained by writing the Supervisor, Chequamegon National Forest, Park Falls, Wisconsin 54552. Smaller Nicolet National Forest is located in the northeast. Maps and hunting

The Wisconsin bird-hunter will find fair-to-good hunting for pheasants, Hungarian partridge, and a few sharp-tailed grouse and bobwhite quail. *Courtesy of Wisconsin Conservation Department.*

information can be obtained from the Supervisor, Nicolet National Forest, Rhinelander, Wisconsin 54501.

With 6.5 million acres of land under its jurisdiction, the state of Wisconsin provides much more public hunting land than does the federal government. An estimated 413,000 acres of this land is in state forests, some of which are almost as large as the national forests. A good example is sprawling Northern Highland State Forest near the northern border of the state. Other state forests include American Legion, Apostle Islands, Black River, Brule River, Flambeau River, Kettle Moraine, and Point Beach. Hunting is permitted on all of the state forests. Of even more importance to the hunter are the 1,178,000 acres of land owned or leased by the Wisconsin Department of Natural Resources. These lands are scattered all over the state.

Full information, including maps, on the state lands can be obtained by writing the Wisconsin Department of Natural Resources, Bureau of Fish and Wildlife Management, Box 450, Madison, Wisconsin 53701. Also ask for their map called *Public Lands Open to Hunting*. It shows all public lands—federal, state, and local—open to hunting.

Surprisingly, county forests, totaling over two million acres, offer more public-hunting lands than either the national forests or state forests. Most are open to public hunting. These are shown on the public-lands map discussed above. Hunting information is available from the Department of Natural Resources.

The timber industry and hydropower companies also own several hundred thousand acres of land, most of which are open to public hunting. The Department of Natural Resources can supply information on these lands, also.

Farmlands support a considerable amount of Wisconsin hunting, and permission is not usually difficult to obtain. All cultivated or enclosed land is automatically posted in Wisconsin, and the hunter needs the owner's permission, either express or implied, to enter it. On other private land, legal posting requires the placing of two signs for every forty acres of land.

Wisconsin's deer hunting rates with the best in the nation. The national, state, and county forests all offer good hunting, as deer are found pretty much all over Wisconsin. Good counties include Waupaca, Jackson, Marinette, Oneida, Iowa, Bayfield, and Wood. Generally, the deer hunting is best in the northern part of the state where there is an abundance of public hunting land.

The black-bear kill in Wisconsin is good, and is best along the northern border. The counties of Bayfield, Forest, Marinette, Ashland, and Sawyer are among the best.

Wisconsin is also one of the best ruffed-grouse states in the nation. The top of the cycle will produce over half a million birds for lucky hunters. Even during low population years, the kill is significant. The Nicolet National Forest in the northeast is one of the top areas in the state. The American Legion State Forest and county forests in this general area are also good. Another good area is the northwest, where big Chequamegon National Forest affords almost unlimited hunting territory. The Northern Highlands State Forest in the north-central part of the state is also good.

While pheasants are widely scattered except for the northern forests, by far the best hunting is in the southern part of the state. The better counties include Columbia, Dane, Grant, Iowa, Kenosha, Lafayette, Racine, Rock, Sauk, and Waukesha, but others in this general area may be equally as good. There are numerous public hunting areas in the prime pheasant range, and they are shown on the public-lands hunting map.

Cottontail rabbits in the south and snowshoes in the north—this is generally the rabbit situation. Gray squirrels are most abundant in the densely forested regions, but the larger fox squirrel prefers the woodlots in the farming country.

Horicon Marsh in Dodge and Fond du Lac Counties is famous for its goose hunting, but geese are bagged just about all over the state. Generally, the duck and goose hunting is good wherever there is water—and there is water just about everywhere in Wisconsin.

As I said, Wisconsin is a land of hunting opportunities.

50 • WYOMING—For Big Game

Wyoming is big—97,914 square miles—and one of our top big-game states. With a population of only 360,000 people, the big western state is sparsely settled and has an abundance of hunting room. Almost half of the big western state, an estimated 32 million acres of mountains and grassy plains, is in the public trust.

The hunter will experience little trouble finding good hunting land in big Wyoming.

Some of the very best antelope, deer, and elk hunting in America can be found in Wyoming. White-tailed deer, as well as mule deer, roam the mountains and plains, and there is a good moose population in the western mountains. The bighorn sheep hunting is good, and mountain goats are hunted sporadically. A struggling grizzly-bear population is completely protected, but black bears are numerous in the mountains, particularly in the northwest.

Mountain lions, coyotes, foxes, bobcats, and a few lynx, badgers, and raccoons are found in Wyoming. They receive very little attention. Lynx are protected.

Hunting for Merriam's turkeys is best in the Black Hills region, with the Laramie Peaks area also good.

Cottontails, snowshoes, and jacks provide plenty of rabbit hunting, and there are a few fox and gray squirrels.

Bird hunters take approximately fifty thousand sage grouse annually, and a fair bag of pheasants. The introduced chukar offers good hunting, and there are a few sharp-tailed grouse, bobwhite quail, and Hungarian partridge. Blue and ruffed grouse are found in the mountains and hill country. Mourning doves are abundant.

Wyoming's national forests offer over nine million acres of hunting land, much of it the best big-game territory in the state.

The largest national forest is 2.5-million-acre Shoshone National Forest, with headquarters in Cody. Wyoming 82414. The supervisor there can furnish maps and hunting information. The Bridger-Teton National Forest, with headquarters at Jackson, Wyoming 83001, provides another 1,700,820 acres. The Bridger portion of the National Forest offers 1,700,000 acres of public hunting. It is also headquartered at Jackson. The headquarters for 1,100,000-acre Medicine Bow National Forest is located at Laramie, Wyoming 82070, while 1,113,000-acre Bighorn National Forest is headquartered at Sheridan, Wyoming 82801.

Not to be overlooked are portions of other national forests that jut into Wyoming. The most popular is the Black Hills National Forest, headquartered in Custer, South Dakota 57730. Idaho's Targhee National Forest extends into western Wyoming. Headquarters are located at St. Anthony, Idaho 83445. The Caribou National Forest with headquarters in Pocatello, Idaho 83201, also extends into the state, and finally, to the south, there is Utah's Wasatch National Forest crossing the border into Wyoming, with headquarters at Salt Lake City, Utah 84101.

The Thunder Basin National Grasslands in the eastern half of the state offer over 600,000 acres of excellent antelope and mule-deer territory. An isolated section of this grasslands is located in prime antelope range in the northeastern part of the state. The Thunder Basin National Grasslands are under the jurisdiction of the Supervisor of the Medicine Bow National Forest. Maps and details are available from that office.

In addition to the national forests and grasslands, there are approximately eighteen million acres of Bureau of Land Management land, much of it fine mule deer and antelope country. The Bureau of Land Management Office at Box 128 Cheyenne, Wyoming 82001, has excellent maps showing all of the lands administered by that agency, as well as other public land in the state. A copy is available for the asking. Also available from the same office are more detailed maps of specific areas.

Lands owned and administered by the various public agencies are sometimes difficult to locate as they are not all well marked. However, a letter to the Wyoming Game and Fish Commission, Box 1589, Cheyenne, Wyoming 82001, will bring a list entitled *Wyoming Game and Fish Commission Land Inventory*. It lists various lands by county and gives acreage and other useful information. Used in conjunction with the Bureau of Land Management maps, it can be helpful.

Attitudes of Wyoming ranchers towards nonresident hunters varies

The author downed this antelope in Wyoming. *Photo by Ginny Gooch.*

tremendously. Collectively, they have been subjected to a good deal of hunting pressure, and the conduct of hunters is not universally good. A hunter entering private land without the permission of the owner is courting trouble.

The Wyoming law requires the hunter to get written permission from a landowner or his agent before entering his land. Some landowners grant permission, some do not, and many charge trespass fees. The Wyoming posting law is a tough one.

Some of the better antelope hunting in Wyoming is on private ranches, and the hunting rights are often leased to licensed guides.

Antelope, mule deer, and elk draw most hunters to Wyoming, and the hunting for these exciting big-game animals is well worth the trip.

An estimated 100,000 antelope roam the eastern plains country. Private ranches, the Thunder Basin National Grasslands, and the vast Bureau of Land Management Lands offer ample hunting opportunities.

Mule deer are found in every county in the big western state. They flourish in both the mountains and plains. Good areas include the Thunder Basin National Grasslands, the Black Hills, Medicine Bow and Bighorn National Forests. These are usually the top areas season after season. The Bureau of Land Management Areas in the same general area are also good. The whitetail hunting is best in the Black Hills National Forest.

The vast national forests are the home of the big elk herds, with Teton rated high, followed by Bighorn and Bridger. Shoshone and Medicine Bow are also good.

While the big-game hunter may fare well on unguided antelope and deer hunts, the services of a good guide are recommended for elk. Wyoming law requres the nonresident hunter to be accompanied by a licensed guide when hunting the wilderness areas of the state.

The Bridger portion of the Bridger-Teton National Forest ranks high as moose territory;, and the Teton and Shoshone National Forests are the best bet for bighorn sheep. Black-bear hunting is best in the northwestern part of Wyoming.

The Bighorn basin offers good pheasant hunting, and sage grouse occur wherever there are substantial sage brush plains.

The small-game and bird hunting is good, but the rich reserves of big game make Wyoming a top hunting state.

Species Index